Routledge Revivals

THE BULWARKS OF PEACE

THE
BULWARKS OF PEACE
AND INTERNATIONAL JUSTICE

BY

HEBER L. HART

Routledge
Taylor & Francis Group

First published in 1918 by Methuen and Co. Ltd.

This edition first published in 2018 by Routledge
2 Park Square, Milton Park, Abingdon, Oxon, OX14 4RN
and by Routledge
52 Vanderbilt Avenue, New York, NY 10017, USA

Routledge is an imprint of the Taylor & Francis Group, an informa business

© 1918 by Taylor and Francis

Publisher's Note
The publisher has gone to great lengths to ensure the quality of this reprint
but points out that some imperfections in the original copies may be
apparent.

Disclaimer
The publisher has made every effort to trace copyright holders and
welcomes correspondence from those they have been unable to contact.
A Library of Congress record exists under ISBN: 77403534

ISBN 13: 978-0-367-14374-9 (hbk)
ISBN 13: 978-0-367-14375-6 (pbk)
ISBN 13: 978-0-429-03169-4 (ebk)

THE BULWARKS OF PEACE

PRESS NOTICES OF FIRST EDITION

THE
BULWARKS OF PEACE
AND INTERNATIONAL JUSTICE

BY

HEBER L. HART, K.C., LL.D.

LATE BRITISH MEMBER OF THE MIXED ARBITRAL TRIBUNALS

NEW AND REVISED EDITION

METHUEN & CO. LTD.
36 ESSEX STREET W.C.
LONDON

First Published . . . . *April 18th 1918*
Second Edition, completely Revised .   *1933*

PREFACE

THERE can be no reasonable doubt that a strong and settled aversion to war is now prevalent among the people of this country. Many may feel only a tepid interest in efforts to maintain international harmony, but few would not be reluctant to become actively involved in belligerent operations consequent upon its disturbance.

It is, however, by no means clear what view is taken by ordinary British citizens as to the kind of measures which those who are in charge of their interests ought to adopt with the object of maintaining peace. But two propositions may be hazarded. (1) A very large majority of the people of Great Britain and Northern Ireland, if they carefully adverted to the matter, would hold that, subject to the maintenance of the security and the just and necessary interests of the Empire, the primary object of British foreign policy should be to keep the United Kingdom from becoming involved in any great war. (2) There would be some difference of opinion as to whether or not the United Kingdom ought ever to engage itself in advance to embark upon war in any given circumstances. But a large majority would hold that it certainly ought not to do so unless it were reasonably clear either (a) that the engagement in that behalf would of itself render it less likely that the United Kingdom would in fact become involved in war than would otherwise be the case ; or (b) that it was the moral duty of the United Kingdom towards the world at large to undertake the engagement because it was an essential feature of what appeared to be the best practicable scheme for the preservation of the general peace.

One must suppose, indeed, that it is clear to every thoughtful citizen that nothing in the whole range of public policy is more important than the prevention of experiences like those of the World War and its consequences. Accordingly no political question is of greater moment than this—how can Great Britain, without any dereliction of its duty, best provide against the occurrence of a like catastrophe ?

A policy of self-reliance and avoidance of engagements which might involve us in wars from which we could otherwise have kept aloof has clearly much in its favour. We might concentrate our energies upon the consolidation of the Empire on a rational and business-like footing, so that it should become not merely a great economic unit, but a true political entity, instead of remaining as it now is a mere congeries of nations sympathetically allied but unconnected by any adequate constitutional organization. We might maintain a strong navy and such other armaments as from time to time were considered reasonably necessary for the defence of our 'free, tolerant and unaggressive' Empire. We might continue to co-operate whole-heartedly with the other members of the League of Nations in all its activities in so far as they did not commit us to measures of armed intervention in their support. And we might disentangle ourselves as soon as possible from any treaty which casts upon us the necessity of going to war in the event of a rupture between other nations not immediately and directly concerning ourselves. Engagements such as those which bound us to declare war in 1914 would thus be absolutely excluded. In these circumstances it would seem unlikely that any foreign state or combination of states would invade the United Kingdom, or its colonies, or any of the Dominions in allegiance to the Crown, so long as they acted in harmony with the British Government. And, notwithstanding the possibility of other dangers, it may surely not unreasonably be felt that we should in this way be able to avoid the horrors of another great war. Accordingly many people will probably sooner or later ask themselves whether on the whole this is not really our wisest course. On the other hand, it may well be that England's age-long habit of actively interesting herself in the affairs of the continent of Europe, and its modern concerns with the regions overseas, really exclude the practicability of this policy. It would, moreover, not improbably be incompatible with the altruistic sentiments of Britons, and indeed might generally be thought to fall short of the standard of Christian ethics which is now rapidly becoming the common and avowed morality of mankind.

Should we then unreservedly throw in our lot with the League of Nations and trust primarily to the co-operation of its member states for our own security as well as for the preservation of the general peace ?

It is obvious that the world as a whole does not yet form a stable society enjoying the sense of general safety under the ægis of this organization. On the contrary, the fact that most of the larger states are at present very far from placing their main reliance upon the League has been demonstrated by the course of disarmament conferences ; the formation of groups with special reference to their own defence, and other developments and tendencies alien to the ' League Spirit,' as well as by the recent hostilities in the Far East. Few, indeed, who have seriously considered the matter will think that, in the present circumstances, the existence of the League as now constituted renders it unnecessary for any Great Power to make its own provision for the security of its territory and its citizens. Some will even feel that the imperfect and tentative confidence which the League has hitherto attracted is in itself a source of danger.

Nor is it surprising that unlimited trust is not

reposed in the renunciation of the right of making war contained in a widely-executed international agreement. It is not unnatural that states should not be prepared to hazard their safety upon the supposition that a government persuaded of the necessity of adopting belligerent measures in order to defend itself from an attack apprehended to be imminent or pretending to be so persuaded, or wanton enough to wish to wage an unnecessary and unrighteous war, would be adequately restrained by the fact of its previous concurrence in this Pact.

The question therefore arises whether it is possible by appropriate amendments in the Covenant to supply the existing deficiencies of the League and so to render it an organization which will be generally regarded as affording the security and assurance of peace which are so urgently necessary.

Security and disarmament are two aspects of what is essentially one subject—the preservation of peace. It is impossible to treat either satisfactorily without at the same time dealing with the other. But if—and only if—the questions to which they give rise can be solved concurrently will peace be effectively established.

In the latter part of this treatise the attempt is made to show that the great desiderata of security and disarmament could be achieved by a covenant on the part of each of the Great Powers to contribute an agreed quota to a collective force and the reduction of its armaments to the level of that quota (except to the extent of any further provision necessary for the purpose of the preservation of internal order). The alterations which would be necessary in the Covenant of the League in order that this scheme should be carried into effect are there considered in detail. Whether there is any prospect of such alterations being made and of the reduction of armaments involved therein is a question for politicians. But the general trend of thought since the outbreak of the Great War and the international agreements for the maintenance of peace in which it has already resulted seem to indicate that schemes which until recently would have appeared to most people Utopian in character may under favourable conditions suddenly become matters of immediate practical politics. The change of attitude with regard to the doctrines of Neutrality is indeed in itself a most striking illustration of the rapidity of advance in world-wide opinion which is now possible. The views propounded in Chapter XIV of this book (which literally reproduces a corresponding chapter of the first edition) were at the time when they were originally published the exact opposite of those which were then still prevalent. Yet already it is evident that they are likely to become the accepted principles of the international jurisprudence of the future.

Whether or not there is in fact any probability of the adoption of the suggested changes in the Covenant of the League the jurist can at all events say with confidence that, without such changes or others essentially similar, the League can never provide a completely trustworthy alternative to the possession of the means of self-defence on the part of each individual Power. In other words, a mutual guarantee of security is the only way of obtaining the degree of disarmament which is in itself necessary for the general security, and conversely disarmament to that extent is the only way of rendering practicable such a guarantee of general security.

If, therefore, Britain is to place its reliance upon the League for its own safety and the maintenance of the general peace, it seems to follow that the United Kingdom must undertake to support the decisions of the League by a certain agreed quota of armed forces. Such a burden, however, in view of the general reduction of armaments which would be an essential feature of any rational scheme providing for such quotas, need not in fact prove excessively onerous.

In this connexion the important point upon which I would venture to insist is this. If the suggested scheme is in practice unattainable, or the United Kingdom decides not to participate in it, we must for our own security rely primarily upon ourselves. In this case considerations of ordinary prudence and good sense seem to indicate the first of the courses which have been referred to above as that which Great Britain should pursue.

A third course, essentially different from either of

the foregoing, has in fact been followed by the statesmen who have administered the British Government in recent years.

They have encouraged, or acquiesced in, the diminution of the constitutional relations between the United Kingdom and the Dominions until they have approached dangerously near to the vanishing point. They have lowered the relative strength of our armaments. They have declined to enter into any general covenant for mutual security with the other members of the League. But at the same time they have signed the Locarno Pact and subsequently advocated the formation of other analogous ' regional treaties.'

Now it is obvious that this Pact has not produced a universal sense of security or resulted in any satisfactory measure of disarmament. But it has reproduced a situation which, so far as the responsibility of Great Britain is concerned, is substantially similar to that which existed in August 1914. The United Kingdom then intervened in the war which had already commenced between four Great Powers because it was bound by treaty to protect the neutrality of Belgium, and also because it felt constrained in honour by some implied understanding with France to range itself upon her side. This intervention involved in its result the utmost strain upon the resources of Britain both in men and materials. The Locarno Pact is framed in language of which the precise import may easily be misconceived, but it seems certain that one of its effects is that if Germany invades France or Belgium, or France invades Germany, Great Britain may have to wage war on behalf of the invaded country.

Whatever then may be the merits of this Pact it seems important to bear in mind certain grave objections which have to be weighed against them.

It contains no limitation of the liability which Great Britain undertakes as a party thereto—no limitation of the number of men or the extent of the armaments which are to be provided in the given contingency, such as would naturally be contained in any covenant for general security and the accompanying scheme of disarmament. Accordingly, having regard to the present state of feeling in this country, it cannot be regarded as by any means certain that, if the contemplated contingency were to arise, the British Government of the day would be able to implement the obligation which has been undertaken in a full and decisive manner. The regular forces of the Crown would no doubt respond without hesitation to the orders which they received. But would there be many volunteers for foreign service ? And if a House of Commons passed a bill for compulsory conscription would its authority survive in sufficient strength to control its execution ? If the answers to these questions should be in the negative, an appalling prospect of national discredit and confusion is opened to the imagination.

Moreover it is to be borne in mind that such a Pact does not make the same appeal to the altruism of mankind as that of the apparently bolder, but in reality more conservative, plan for the general security of all. At the same time, from the nature of the case, no regional agreement can establish even the security of the parties thereto. If then the matter is to be considered simply as one to be determined by considerations of self-regarding prudence, it seems probable that the ordinary citizen upon calm consideration would not think it worth the while of this nation to have undertaken the far-reaching risks which are involved in this treaty. Whether indeed its implications are generally appreciated would seem doubtful.

In these circumstances I feel that it is now as important as it ever was before that the electors of the United Kingdom should have sound and clear ideas about the League of Nations. No one can be expected to acquaint himself with any large proportion of the voluminous literature issued by the League and individual authors concerning its functions and activities. It is, however, quite possible to state with brevity and simplicity all the essential principles and relevant facts which are necessary for an adequate appreciation of the relation of the League to the practical problem of the maintenance of peace.

The first edition of this treatise was written in 1917 with the object of demonstrating, as the result of a review of the principles of the regulation of human conduct, the essential conditions of an effective League of Peace. These conditions were to a large extent embodied in the Covenant of the League of Nations. Indeed a former President of the Permanent Court of International Justice, writing to me in 1925, went so far as to say :—'In reading your book I was struck by the fact that all you preached in '17 became realised in '19.'

The continuing interest of the work was indicated by the publication in 1926 by the Austrian state press of a translation of its original text into the German language by Dr. Gustav Walker, Professor and Dean of the Faculty of Law and Political Science in the University of Vienna.

It has accordingly appeared to me that a new edition consisting largely of the fresh matter rendered necessary by the situation as it now exists, but preserving the original plan so far as practicable, may prove useful.

I would add that I have not written from the point of view of an advocate of any particular course of policy. My primary object has been to demonstrate as succinctly as possible the principles governing the maintenance of peace and order, and the essential elements of international jurisprudence. In this connexion, however, I have thought it of the greatest practical importance to indicate the changes which must be made in the constitution and powers of the existing League of Nations if it is to become an organisation for the prevention of war upon which humanity can safely rely

HEBER HART

THE TEMPLE
August 1933

CONTENTS

INTRODUCTION

IN every department of science or art there are fundamental principles and facts upon which its students and professors alike proceed. No problem, indeed, can be studied effectively without some previous acquaintance with the subject in connexion with which it arises. And if we seek to ascertain the best means of securing peace it is well that we should keep in view the elements of social order. We ought to take into consideration the relation of war to the evolution of humanity; the causes of wars in modern times; the reasons for the difficulty of entirely eliminating or completely counteracting these causes; the influences and forces whereby men living in communities are inclined or constrained to orderly behaviour, and the extent to which these influences and forces are applicable to nations and states; the scope of general rules and administrative ordinances respectively in relation to social order; the nature and practical value of International Law; the essential sanction of right; the social function of force; the interdependence of states; the position of the Great Powers; and the special functions of the League of Nations in relation to world-order.

Many manuals of war have been written: this little work is a Primer of Peace. It is an attempt to provide a compendious statement of the material facts and guiding principles which should be borne in mind by any one who is considering what ought to be done by the governments and peoples of the various states of the world with the object of preventing the outbreak of wars in the future.

The practical aspect of the problem of the maintenance of peace has been fundamentally altered by the great fact of the existence of the League of Nations. Since its creation it has naturally been the centre of the activities of those who have been anxious for peace. The attention of the world has been focussed upon its work. To a large extent all new suggestions and speculations with regard to the means of avoiding war must now, as it were, start from the position which the League occupies. Theoretically, the essential conditions of order and peace are the same to-day as they were in 1914. But the practical questions which have since arisen in this connexion have necessarily assumed a new form.

The constitution of the League of Nations by the voluntary agreement of nearly all the separate states among which the human race is distributed, may justly be regarded as the greatest political achievement of mankind. The Covenant is the Magna Charta of world-order and international justice. It recognizes the existence of a universal society and the interdependence of all its members, whom it binds together in a union for the common good of all.

There is now habitual personal intercourse between the statesmen of the various Powers. A

World Conference is in effect in permanent session. The decision of most international disputes by a disinterested Council or Court has been rendered practicable. And the formation of a public opinion prevailing from Pole to Pole and its articulate expression are now possible.

The prestige of the League as a body existing primarily for the maintenance of peace is reinforced by the beneficent activities which it carries on for the general welfare of mankind. Conceived as an entity to prevent war it has developed into a body for the promotion of the enjoyment of peace.

The best ideas of the various nations with regard to matters of hygiene, labour conditions, education, economics, and other branches of social science are carried to a common forum by their representatives ; are there improved by the discussions of friendly colleagues, and thereafter diffused throughout the earth for the advantage of all.

When the joint action of the different governments is necessary for the common interest the appropriate conventions are negotiated with comparative facility. The means of traffic and intercommunication can be improved to the greatest possible degree ; and social evils are combated with constantly increasing success.

Incidentally, moreover, it seems not improbable that the work of the League, regarded as a whole, will lead in the course of time to the rationalization and assimilation of the divers national laws of the various countries of the globe.

The work accomplished by the League is recorded and summarized in its official publications. In this connexion it is sufficient here to say that one cannot reasonably be disappointed with its results up to the present time. No civilized nation has yet succeeded in entirely preventing crimes within its own borders, or by any means perfected its criminal code or even its form of government. Naturally the prevention of war and the establishment of international organization and control are tasks which will not be completed quickly or easily.

On the whole it is quite clear that the position which the League occupies marks a signal advance in human development. The extent of this may be suggested by imagining the reception which would have been given so late as the middle of 1914 to a proposal to establish an international organization with the functions which the League is now exercising, and comparing it with the attitude which at the present time actually prevails with regard to the League over a large part of the world and particularly in Europe.

The League has had to face grave dangers ; it has seemed impotent in the face of some troubles ; its credit has at times appeared to be declining. Nevertheless, the essential grandeur of its constitution and purpose ; the progress which it has already made ; and the firm hold which it has established upon the sympathies and even upon the affections of a vast body of thoughtful people, justify the conviction that the conscience and the intelligence of mankind will never suffer its permanent paralysis or destruction. On the contrary, the attainment of its full development will be the consummation towards which humanity will henceforth strive with constant hope and patient effort, realizing that it might well ensure to mankind all the individual happiness which their moral and intellectual development should render possible.

It is, however, clear that the League in its present form is not by any means completely equipped for the satisfactory attainment of the principal object for which it exists. It is, therefore, of paramount importance to ascertain the changes which must be made in the Covenant, if the League is to be a really efficient alternative to the existing means of self-protection on the part of the several Powers respectively.

As at present constituted, the League, in two respects of supreme moment, fails to afford an adequate security for peace. 1. It does not provide an effective method for the settlement of disputes arising out of demands based upon justice or necessity for the alteration of existing conditions or relations between states and peoples. 2. It does not provide an executive power upon which the League can rely for the practical enforcement of its will for peace.

Many will look for a remedy for these defects to the establishment of a federated commonwealth embracing the entire world, or to constitutional arrangements which would, in their practical effect, involve the existence of such a world-state. For reasons, however, which are discussed in Chapter IV., it is clear that an organization of this nature is not, for the time being at all events, within the scope of practical politics. It is possible that the conception of such a federation may usefully be entertained as an ideal—as the ultimate solution of the great problem of universal peace. Nevertheless, it seems open to doubt whether in circumstances and under conditions in which a universal state would be possible, its formal constitution would any longer be necessary.

Meanwhile the practical reformer has to work out a different solution—a form of international organization intermediate between the League of Nations in its present stage of development and the ideal conception of the world-state. In other words, the present task of the reformer is to ascertain the changes in the Covenant of the League which are essential for its efficiency and at the same time are possible of attainment in the immediate future.

From the experience of past ages many principles of warfare have been evolved. From the like experience it is possible also to ascertain the essential principles of order and peace.

In the last three chapters of this book the attempt is made to deal specifically with the changes in the Covenant of the League, which ought to be supported by states which intend to rely upon its existence, and the efficient exercise of its functions, for their own security and the maintenance of the general peace. But the complete argument which results in the views there advanced is progressively presented by the contents of the work as a whole.

THE BULWARKS OF PEACE

CHAPTER I

THE GREAT ASCENT

SECTION I

FROM ANARCHY TO GOODWILL

IF we look back steadily upon all that is known to us of the nature and condition of mankind in past times and then review justly the state and apparent tendencies of the race at the present day we shall hardly fail to discern the track of a spiritual ascent. Our vision cannot reach downwards to the immeasurable depths of the beginning of the stupendous journey; and the goal of its completion is still hidden in the secret places of destiny. But from the outlines which are faintly traceable of the earliest stage which is at all within our ken and the trend of the progress which has been since maintained we may well infer that men began their life upon this planet in the abysmal darkness of anarchy and that they will never cease to struggle upward until they reach the genial atmosphere of a universal commonwealth of goodwill.

It is true that this great objective is still so far above us that we cannot even form a clear and definite conception of the conditions which would prevail in a society of human beings entirely emancipated from the dominion of force—a society in which the life of every one should be regulated by the gentle sway of a beneficent conscience. But already it would seem that the inhabitants of the earth, regarded generally, are not so far below the standard of such a community as they are above that of the world as it was during the earliest period of the existence of our race. In any case the past must be compared carefully with the present if we are to have an adequate perception of the promise of the future.

The habits and disposition of human beings at the time of the origin of their species cannot of course be ascertained with precision or certainty. But, from the data at our command, we may infer that they were speechless creatures, devoid of self-consciousness, incapable of reasoning, and without any definite perception of right or wrong ; and that they were dependent for the maintenance of existence solely upon the use of their bodily organs.[1] They must indeed have been so utterly unlike the men of to-day that they elude our apprehension altogether. It is impossible even for imagination to reconstruct a credible picture of their daily lives. It is, however, only reasonable to suppose that the farther we could penetrate backward into the history of our ancestors the more humbly endowed we should find them. Only the eye of omniscience could have discerned in primitive men the germs of humanity as we know it now.

When, after the passage of ages, the faculty of articulated speech had been acquired the development of reason became possible and the intellectual

[1] See Romanes' *Mental Evolution in Man* (1888), pp. 345-7.

advance of mankind began. But the evidence of language itself indicates that a vast period must have elapsed after its use had been acquired before morality and conscience were evolved. A close examination of words, 'those oldest prehistoric testimonies,' reveals the fact that all moral notions contain something morally indifferent. The words indicating good and evil had originally no moral import. They are metaphorical extensions of the meaning of words which originally had only material significations. Thus 'right' means straight and 'wrong' twisted. 'This seems to show that language is older than morality'—that it dates from a period when a moral judgment, a knowledge of good and evil, had not yet dawned in the human mind. Had the ideas of good and evil and of right and wrong been innate it would naturally have followed that we should have had original words for them.[1]

When we pass on towards the close of the prehistoric period we are able to recognize the men and women of whom we there catch dim and distant glimpses as fellow-creatures of our own. But we find that their characters were still unsocial and their lives comparatively speaking isolated.

'If,' said Sir Henry Maine,[2] 'I were attempting, for the more special purposes of the jurist, to express compendiously the characteristics of the situation in which mankind disclose themselves at the dawn of their history, I should be satisfied to quote a

[1] Romanes, *Mental Evolution in Man*, citing Geiger, pp. 346–7 ; Lord Avebury, citing Emerson, in *Origin of Civilisation*, 6th ed. pp. 421, 425.
[2] *Ancient Law* (Sir F. Pollock's (1930) ed.), pp. 141–2.

few verses from the Odyssey of Homer. . . . " They have neither assemblies for consultation nor *Themistes*, but every one exercises jurisdiction over his wives and his children, and they pay no regard to one another." These lines are applied to the Cyclops, and it may not perhaps be an altogether fanciful idea when I suggest that the Cyclops is Homer's type of an alien and less advanced civilization ; for the almost physical loathing which a primitive community feels for men of widely different manners from its own usually expresses itself by describing them as monsters, such as giants or even (which is almost always the case in Oriental mythology) as demons. However that may be, the verses condense in themselves the sum of the hints which are given us by legal antiquities. Men are first seen distributed in perfectly insulated groups, held together by obedience to the parent. Law is the parent's word.'

But ' whether we have regard to actual history, to tradition, to antiquarian remains, or flint implements, we obtain uniform evidence of a continuous process of upward development.' [1]

It is not necessary for the present purpose to attempt to trace the painful progress of human civilization. It is sufficient to glance at its results as we now see them.

' What a piece of work is a man ! How noble in reason ! how infinite in faculties ! in form and moving how express and admirable ! in action how like an angel ! in apprehension how like a god ! the beauty of the world ! the paragon of animals ! ' [2]

[1] Romanes' *Mental Evolution in Man* (1888), p. 390.
[2] *Hamlet*, ii. 2.

It is truly an immeasurable distance which separates the intelligence of men whose voices reach across the oceans and whose hands can weigh the very stars from that of their mute and groping ancestors of the primeval world.

When, however, we consider the social and moral nature of mankind, we discern the results of a progress which is more wonderful still.

Man, as we now know him, has the faculty of discriminating between right and wrong. There is an active principle in his soul whereby, when two alternative courses are presented to his mind, he feels an obligation to select the one which he perceives to be in conformity with the right. By this characteristic quality of his conscience man is completely differentiated from the brutes.

It is true that there is not yet a correspondence which approaches at all closely to uniformity in men's perceptions of the right and that each individual may from time to time find it difficult or even impossible to perceive the obligation incumbent upon him in the circumstances of a particular situation. Nor, owing to the gradual development of the faculty of conscience, the continued insistency of the animal desires of mankind, the limitations of intelligence, and the complicated and varying conditions of social life, could it well be otherwise. And accordingly many philosophers have done much to depreciate the substantive importance of this faculty in the eyes of ordinary men by insisting upon its entire dependence upon the effects of education, the association of ideas, the perception of utility, or a particular form of belief in the unseen. It is, however, important to lay firm hold upon the outstanding truth that, so far as regards historic times, conscience is the essential fact of human existence—the supreme and distinctive quality of mankind—the fundamental element upon which society depends. It is the Alpha and the Omega of moral progress.

It would seem that the extent of the dominion of conscience has been steadily increasing ever since the dawn of civilization. When men first awoke to the sense of duty its scope was probably limited to their conduct in relation to members of their own family or tribe. But at the present time it is manifest that, in the case of all the more advanced races, conscience takes cognizance of duty to mankind at large. There can indeed be comparatively few sane and educated people now living in the civilized world who would not recognize that in certain circumstances any human being might have a claim upon their consideration.

It is not of course practicable to measure accurately the extent of the moral progress which mankind have accomplished hitherto. But certain salient facts go far as indications of the present position.

The great majority of human beings now live in large communities. Order normally prevails throughout the several social aggregates. Taking the world as a whole, tranquillity is the rule; violence is the exception. Most people observe the laws and customs of their respective countries willingly, and usually without consciously adverting to the sanctions by which they are enforced. Aliens and strangers are protected by governments and generally treated with courtesy by the citizens of the states in which they are temporarily resident.

A difference between right and wrong is everywhere assumed ; and conduct which is wrong is for the most part recognized as a deviation from the ordinary course of affairs. All civilized men are capable of understanding the precept : ' Whatsoever ye would that men should do to you do ye even so to them.' By a large proportion of mankind this precept is felt to be obligatory. Many seriously endeavour to follow it in practice ; and people who in the main succeed in doing so are to be found everywhere, and everywhere in the long run are regarded with admiration and affection. So obvious indeed has the essential harmony of good-nature with the conditions of social life become that even those who are selfish and unjust themselves are generally disposed to prefer that better qualities should be cultivated by others. In short, already the dominion of the social sense is far more extensive than that of brutish ferocity and irrational hatred. Already we can almost imagine that there might be a society of morally perfect men : for people who at least suggest that conception figure in the records of history and are encountered in ever increasing numbers in contemporary life.

If then it is to be assumed that man commenced his career entirely under the dominion of selfish impulses, when we review his present moral condition it seems reasonable to anticipate that he will ultimately attain a state in which he will be under the complete direction of an elevated conscience.

A particular nation may have grounds for gloomy forebodings and doubts as to the continuance of its own advance along the upward path of social progress. But in the contemplation of the future of the human race collectively an optimistic view is the necessary result of an adequate perception of the true relation of the present to the past.[1]

The instincts which men have shared so long with wild and savage animals have naturally been manifested in selfishness and cruelty. Naturally also the supremacy of the developed conscience will in the fullness of time ensure the prevalence of sympathy and goodwill.

Section II

FROM WAR TO PEACE

It seems probable that, for a very long period after men had become capable of rational communication with one another, their state of life continued to be anarchical and that in any relations into which they were from time to time brought together unregulated force had free play. Outside the narrow limits of their family groups they were reciprocally hostile. Conflict was the usual result of the contact of one group with another. Existence passed in isolation varied by strife.

Accordingly man had to achieve his great ascent to a very large extent by means of war. The general belligerency of the race brought about its own partial remedy; for the earliest social order seems to have been indirectly due to war. War

[1] ' I remain persuaded,' said the late Lord Avebury, ' that the past history of man has, on the whole, been one of progress, and that, in looking forward to the future, we are justified in doing so with confidence and with hope' (*Origin of Civilisation*, 6th ed. p. 552).

caused the union of family groups into larger groups, and again the coalescence of these groups into still larger aggregates ; and in this way it promoted peace and order between the individuals who thus became associated in the enlarged communities. Internal peace was purchased at the price of external war. In a sense civilized states are the result of the travail of humanity in barbaric strife.

'Coherence,' said Herbert Spencer, 'is first given to small hordes of primitive men during combined opposition to enemies. . . . At first the unions exist only for military purposes. Each component society retains for a long time its independent internal administration, and it is only when joint action in war has become habitual that the cohesion is made permanent by a common political organization.'[1] 'Everywhere the wars between societies originate governmental structures, and are causes of all such improvements in those structures as increase the efficiency of corporate action against environing societies.'[2]

But throughout the greater part of the historical period, except so far as strife was excluded by the effects of these processes of coalescence or absorption, war remained the normal condition of mankind. The communities into which men were divided, even after they had attained a size and degree of internal order entitling them to the character of states, so far as they came into contact, were habitually antagonistic in their relations with one another. To the citizen of one state the citizen of another state was normally an enemy. The

[1] *Principles of Sociology*, vol. ii. pp. 278, 279.
[2] *Ibid.* vol. i. p. 540.

formation of great empires from time to time enlarged the areas within which internal peace prevailed ; but these empires themselves were for the most part at war with other peoples. No condition approaching that of a stable equilibrium between independent states was indeed practicable until civilization had attained a very advanced stage. History, until it reaches comparatively modern times, is in the main a narrative of wars.

In the realm of thought the evils attendant upon defeat in war must always have been recognized. But so long as fighting and the preparations for carrying it on were among the chief concerns and interests of life, and martial prowess passed for the supreme glory of mankind, it is not to be supposed that ordinary people would regard war in itself as an evil. The revolt of the human soul against the carnage of the battle-field and the holocaust of homesteads could proceed only *pari passu* with the moral advancement of mankind. Only in proportion as men became more sympathetic with their fellows and more interested in the sufferings of others did they concern themselves with the distinction between a just and an unjust war and with the means of preventing wars altogether. In a word, the increasing aversion from war and preference for peace is only one aspect of the progress of the race from the nature of the brute towards that of the perfect man.

Naturally with regard to war, as with regard to conduct generally, great thinkers and moral teachers often proved themselves far in advance of their contemporaries. Even thousands of years ago ever and anon some voice was raised in an effort to impress upon mankind the more elevated and essentially reasonable view.

Thus Micah, the Hebrew prophet, foretelling the conduct of men in a happier age than his own, wrote : ' They shall beat their swords into plow-shares, and their spears into pruning-hooks : nation shall not lift up a sword against nation, neither shall they learn war any more. But they shall sit every man under his vine and under his fig tree ; and none shall make them afraid.' [1]

Plato, Aristotle, Sallust, and many others of the wise men of Greece and Rome, clearly perceived and boldly proclaimed that war should be carried on only for the sake of peace.[2] ' Wars,' said Cicero, ' are to be undertaken for this end, that we may live in peace without being injured. . . . In engaging in war we ought to make it appear that we have no other view but peace.' [3]

And no one will overlook the influence of Christianity in inculcating the virtues which in practice tend naturally to goodwill and peace.

It is not necessary here to trace in detail the progress of thought upon this subject. Some of the more important of the attempts which have been made by eminent publicists to enlist the sympathies of mankind in the cause of peace will be referred to in other parts of this treatise. It is sufficient to point out in this place that, for many years past, the numbers of those who have been

---

[1] Micah iv. 3, 4. Cp. Isaiah ii. 4.

[2] Plato's *De Legibus*, lib. i. p. 628 of Stephens' ed. ; Aristotle's *Politics*, vii. 14, 15 ; Sallust's *Epist. I. Ad C. Cæsarem*, p. 345 of ed. Gottlieb Cortii.

[3] *De Officiis*, translation by C. R. Edmonds (Bohn's Classical Library), i. 11, 23.

writing and working with the express object of preventing wars have continually and vastly increased.

Moreover, as the world has grown older wars
have in fact steadily diminished in frequency. If,
for example, we compare the records of the years
between 1815 and 1914 with those of any earlier
period of the same length, we shall see that peace
prevailed between the various peoples of the earth
to a greater extent after the battle of Waterloo than
it had ever done before.

It was indeed natural that this should have been
so. The governments and citizens of the leading
countries were, for the most part, in a higher state
of moral development in the nineteenth century than
in earlier times. Accordingly, in the course of that
century a disposition towards unjustifiable aggression
was manifested less frequently than before. The
representatives of different states were drawn more
closely together in friendly intercourse, while the
commercial relations between the inhabitants of
divers parts of the world were greatly developed.
Disputes between governments of a kind which
in previous centuries would have resulted in strife
were in many instances adjusted by diplomatic
negotiation before they had reached a critical stage,
and in some instances even after that point had
been passed. There was also an increasing disposition on the part of statesmen to submit their
controversies to the reasoned decision of impartial
minds.

Many disputes, including several of an undoubtedly
menacing character, were thus peaceably adjusted
by arbitration. By the latter part of the century,
indeed, the precedents for this course had become

so numerous in certain kinds of controversies, particularly those regarding boundaries and claims to indemnities, that in such cases arbitration had become the established form of procedure as between many states. The facilities for obtaining a satisfactory adjudication by this means were, moreover, rapidly being improved. It had, in fact, become apparent that a standing tribunal, constituted in such a way as to command general confidence and open to all who might be willing to resort to it, afforded as to most disputes a beneficent alternative to war analogous to the remedy afforded by ordinary municipal tribunals in lieu of the duel and other forms of self-redress.

During that century also the Powers acted in concert to a greater extent than had ever been the case before.

From 1815 until 1914 Britain, indeed, was only once engaged in a war with another great Power; and whether or not the conflict with Russia ought to have been avoided has been a matter of controversy among Englishmen ever since its commencement.

And in the early part of the year 1914 it seems fairly safe to say that there was throughout the Empire a general disposition towards peace. Probably never before had so large a proportion of the electorate of the United Kingdom been decidedly averse from war and firmly bent upon industrial progress and the social improvement of the community. It is true that Britain might still, for a time at all events, have remained at peace, and that, nevertheless, she, upon her own initiative, declared war against Germany. But it is also true that it was believed by her own citizens generally, as well as by the large majority of well-informed neutrals, that, in taking the course which she did, Britain was faithfully discharging a stern and terrible duty and fulfilling a solemn obligation as a trustee of civilization. No unprejudiced and instructed observer could regard the action of the United Kingdom as in itself a disturbance of the peace, or as in any way inconsistent with a due regard for the importance of avoiding war. Accordingly, so far as the British Empire is concerned, the events of August 1914 and their consequences afford no evidence whatever that the hatred of war and the love of peace, which previously had been steadily increasing, had then sustained an even momentary check.

At the present time, moreover, there can be no reasonable doubt that, largely as a result of the Great War, there is throughout the world a more general and intense aversion to armed strife than ever existed at any previous epoch. The vast majority of civilized men now not only regard peaceful relations between the various states of the world as normal, but clearly realize that even an occasional war may be a truly terrible calamity. They accordingly perceive that grave moral guilt attaches to those who draw the sword except upon the clearest necessity and in pursuance of a sense of duty. They are consequently willing to entertain any suggestions directed to the establishment of a lasting peace which may appear to be reasonable and practical.

The very fact that henceforth, if war is waged, the belligerents may employ means of causing far more extensive destruction and suffering than could be effected by any which were available in previous wars, is in itself calculated to strengthen and perpetuate the reluctance to disturb the peace. And so long as the impression made by the events of the colossal strife of the Great War remains vivid in the minds of men we may feel assured that the spirit of humanity will be sternly resolved that no similar evil shall afflict the race.

Having regard to the foregoing considerations we may justly feel confident that wars of any kind will prove fewer and farther between as time rolls on.

In particular, genuine disputes of a justiciable nature or at all analogous thereto will almost always be settled peaceably. Unless either party wishes for war, the state which asserts what it believes to be a definite right recognized by a pre-existing standard of justice and the state which denies that right, will both alike perceive that the issue between them ought to be determined by negotiation, mediation, arbitration, or some other peaceable process.

It is indeed a cardinal and manifest truth in this connexion that the moral progress of mankind involves an increasing tendency towards peace.

'Nature guarantees the coming of perpetual peace, through the natural course of human propensities : not indeed with sufficient certainty to enable us to prophesy the future of this ideal theoretically, but yet clearly enough for practical purposes. And thus this guarantee of nature makes it a duty that we should labour for this end, an end which is no mere chimera.' [1]

[1] Kant's *Perpetual Peace*, translated by Miss M. Campbell Smith, p. 157.

The increase of goodwill on the part of men towards one another as individuals, by which hostility and indifference are being steadily banished from human society, involves a corresponding amelioration of the mutual relations of the separate political communities among which the race is distributed. States themselves, though somewhat more tardily than individuals, are passing away from the epoch of anarchy and hostility towards a social condition of prevailing goodwill and peace.

PROPOSITION I.—The natural progress of mankind involves the development of a social conscience which will ultimately secure the prevalence of goodwill and peace.

CHAPTER II

THE REAL DANGERS

IN order that those who desire to make effective provision against the outbreak of wars should attain the greatest possible measure of success, it is necessary that they should appreciate the causes from which, in the absence of such provision, wars would be likely to arise. Until quite recently these causes have generally been for the most part overlooked by those who have hitherto propounded schemes for the establishment of perpetual peace.

War was often regarded as the litigation of states. This partial and inexact conception of its nature is closely associated with the assumption that all the differences and difficulties which may hereafter arise between states will be susceptible of satisfactory settlement by the application of rules of International Law, and, accordingly, that arbitration in accordance therewith should prove a complete, as well as efficient, substitute for war. It is of the greatest importance to recognize clearly at the outset of an inquiry such as is pursued in this treatise that this assumption is untenable. Only when this is perceived can we be in a position to apply our minds steadily to the grave difficulties of the matter in hand and at the same time be secure against the risk of pursuing a dangerous illusion.

Many wars have been due to genuine disputes or controversies between two or more states as to their respective rights or duties under rules generally recognized as obligatory or in accordance with the provisions of a particular treaty.   In any such case war having been a method of pursuing a claim based upon an alleged right under a pre-existing rule may be said to have borne a certain resemblance to an action at law.   This being so the important consequence is naturally observed that arbitration would have been an appropriate and effective substitute for war.   And we have seen in the preceding chapter that there is good ground for hoping that henceforth controversies of this character will in fact be settled by arbitration or some other cognate process.

Most wars of the past, however, by reason of their causes and the objects of the belligerents, have borne no real analogy to litigation.   And, if wars arise in the future, it is probable that they also will bear no such analogy ; or, at all events, that they will arise from difficulties for which International Law, as at present understood, provides no solution, and for which arbitration, or any similar method of decision, according to a standard of right already recognized, would be no remedy at all.

International Law is a system of rules which purports to govern the relations of states.   It ignores the existence of nations.

In all regions of the world where settled government exists, every inhabitant, speaking generally, is both a member of a nation and a citizen of a state.

A nation, or people, or race, is a ' large number of

human beings, united together by a common language,[1] and by similar customs and opinions, resulting usually from common ancestry, religion, and historical circumstances.'[2]

A state is a community bound together by a common political allegiance.

'A state may be co-extensive with one people . . . or may embrace several. . . . One people may enter into the composition of several states.'[3]

The collective affairs of human beings are managed by the governments of the states to which they belong. The government of a state is the organ by which its citizens collectively communicate with the citizens of another state through the government of the latter. The inhabitants of the civilized world, moreover, generally recognize the implications of the fact that they are grouped into separate states and that the world consists of a society of states. A nation as such is, according to established custom, inarticulate; and it is assumed indeed to be incapable of relations with a state or with another nation.[4]

It follows that, at all events as a matter of form, war is made by states and not by nations. A breach of the peace between inhabitants of adjacent countries, if it were not followed by war between the

---

[1] This is generally but not universally the case.

[2] Holland's *Jurisprudence*, 13th ed. p. 46. Prof. Holland speaks of a 'people'; but the present writer adopts his language as equally applicable to the word 'nation,' which is perhaps more commonly used in the present connexion.

[3] Holland's *Jurisprudence*, 13th ed. p. 46.

[4] The provisions made by various post-war instruments for the protection of minorities should, however, be borne in mind in this connexion.

states to which they respectively belonged, would be regarded by statesmen and jurists merely as a lawless outbreak to be repressed according to the criminal code of one or other of those states.

The relations between states are then of cardinal and exclusive importance in respect of the final issue of war or peace. But the relations between nations, although indefinite and not normally susceptible of jural recognition, may in fact determine the relations of states.

Nations are living organisms. As such they are necessarily involved in continual change ; but there is no uniformity in the ways in which they severally change. Differences between them in respect of nature and environment, with the consequent actions and reactions of the one upon the other, result in vast differences in the changes which the nations themselves undergo. Accordingly, they vary relatively as well as absolutely. While one increases in numbers and strength, another declines. While one is being born, another may be dying.

The nations are the physical bases upon which the states exist. Owing, therefore, to the varying changes in the nations, the states themselves are constantly changing in their respective populations and relative power. The people of one state may be pressing upon its borders with a powerfully expansive tendency, while that of a neighbouring state is steadily declining in numbers. The wealth and military strength of the former may be increasing by leaps and bounds, while the spirit and the resources of the latter are falling below the level which they reached in the days when its territory was acquired.

Changes in nations also lead to changes in states in another and very different way. The function of the state is to enable the nation to realize itself in social life—to provide it with the political structure necessary to internal order and to its corporate solidarity in relation to the external world. Accordingly, where a state fails to perform this function properly and with satisfaction to the people concerned, a tendency towards change is sooner or later created which in the long run may affect the society of states at large.

Where, for example, a nation is distributed among two or more states, although the sense of solidarity between its several portions may for centuries have lain almost dormant, the racial spirit may gradually awake to a realization of its common nationality. If then the mutual attraction and the desire for political coalescence rise into activity and power, the relations between the states concerned naturally become disturbed and ultimately altered. Or where, again, a nation, or part of a nation, is comprised, together with another people, within one and the same state, the former may become impatient for a separate political existence. Here also the realization of the national aspiration can be attained only by means of an alteration in the composition of the society of states.

It follows that there is a physical or natural basis for a constantly operating tendency to change in the relations and territorial extent of the various states of the world. The changes in the absolute and relative strength of nations and the spirit of nationality in its rise or fall are continually setting up tendencies to disturbance of the order which for the time being exists in the society of states, and thus preventing the establishment of a condition of stable equilibrium.

Accordingly we find that, ever since states were first formed, the political geography of the world has been constantly changing and the balance of power shifting. The boundaries of the various empires, kingdoms, and republics, as well as their relative strength, have been varying throughout the whole of the historical period. If maps, showing the territorial distribution of the states of Europe, or of the world, at the end of each century, say even for the last five hundred years, be compared, the vast extent of the changes which have been taking place will at once be apparent. ' The history of states is a history not of permanence but of change ; and in this respect, whilst they continue to be composed of human elements, the future will not differ from the past.' [1]

Nevertheless, strange as it may seem, there has been a persistent disposition on the part of those who have laboured for the preservation of peace to overlook the natural necessity which from time to time arises for territorial readjustments.

This oversight is, for example, observable in the scheme for the prevention of wars which was ascribed by Sully to Henry the Fourth of France. ' In aiming at . . . a new *status quo* which should be final, it sinned against nature. . . . The contrast between the distribution of power and of territory which he imagined, and that which actually resulted from the action of the latent forces which he failed to observe, proved how little he was in a con-

[1] Lorimer's *Law of Nations*, vol. ii. p. 200.

dition either to anticipate or to control the rise and fall of states. . . . In the frequent enumerations of the existing states which occur in Sully's pages, moreover, it is instructive to observe that Prussia, even in its incipient form of the Duchy of Brandenburg, is not once mentioned.' [1]

So also, when a new arrangement of territories has been made or ratified, there has usually been an express or implied assumption on the part of the states concerned that it was intended to be permanent. ' The *status quo* established at Münster, at Utrecht, at Luneville, at Vienna, at Paris, at Berlin, were all to be permanent; and as their permanence was guaranteed by the doctrine of the balance of power, it is not difficult to see how that doctrine came to be, in itself, a perpetual *casus belli*.' [2] The difficulties which have already arisen with regard to some of the territorial arrangements contained in the treaties made at the conclusion of the Great War will naturally occur to the reader in this connexion.

It is then necessary that we should recognize the theory of the permanence of territorial arrangements as a conventional fiction and take into account fully the plain truth that changes in nations due to natural causes will continue to cause changes in the society of states. In other words, changes *de facto* in nations will in some way or other be followed by changes *de jure* in states.

Hitherto changes in territorial arrangements have for the most part been effected at the cost of

---

[1] Lorimer's *Law of Nations*, vol. ii. pp. 218, 219.
[2] *Ibid.* pp. 200–1.

war ; although in modern times Congresses of the Powers and the Concert of Europe, as well as voluntary agreements, have also played a very considerable part in bringing them about.

In this connexion it is of paramount importance to recognize that International Law, as we shall see hereafter, makes no adequate provision for giving effect to the operation of the natural causes from which the necessity for territorial readjustments arises. So far as it relates to the acquisition of territory, it largely consists of rules of the Roman Civil Law applied to the relations of states. It takes no cognizance of the existence of nations or of the constant changes which they undergo and which prevent the society of states from assuming the stability of form which is in itself necessary in order that the operation of general rules may be thoroughly effective.

It may be that natural changes of the kind which we have been considering will gradually diminish in the relative magnitude of their importance. But it cannot reasonably be doubted that they will long continue to operate to such an extent that occasionally the consequent changes in the relations of states *de facto* will have to be recognized by territorial and other readjustments of their respective positions. Here then is a pregnant cause of future wars, unless the political machinery of the world be specially adapted for the purpose of preventing them.

Economic requirements must also be borne in mind as possible causes of war. Among these are the want of access to the sea or to the sources of the supply of raw materials. Excessively irritating restrictions upon trade may also operate in the same direction.

In connexion with the causes of wars, we must also take into consideration ambition and the lust of territory on the part of those in control of the power of great states. The changes which occur naturally in the relative strength and spirit of nations have too often provided the opportunity for aggression and the temptation to injustice and violence. If the relative strength of nations could have been kept stable, the states existing at any given time might, as it were, once and for all, have fought out the question of their respective pretensions. As it has in fact been, the constant natural changes in the nations have given occasion for recurring uncertainty as to the actual distribution of might among the various states.[1]

Thus from time to time it has happened that some nation, on reaching a period of special racial development, with a rapidly increasing population and accumulating wealth and resources, has felt itself, whether justly or not, hampered by confinement within territorial limits which have no longer satisfied its aspirations. Under such circumstances its rulers have only too easily emancipated themselves from the ordinary restraints of moral principles. The cause of national aggrandizement has been erected into a special and, as it were, transcendental standard of right, and for this cause the political leaders of the state have become

[1] ' It is the necessity of ascertaining on each special occasion the side on which might really lies, and the possibility of the temporary triumph of ultimate weakness, that is the cause of international war ' (Lorimer's *Law of Nations*, vol. ii. p. 208).

not only willing but anxious to fight. With the coming of a favourable opportunity, or the occurrence of a plausible pretext, the state has wished for war. In such a case the friendly mediation of third parties could have been only an embarrassment of a temporary character. Arbitration would have been equally inapplicable. Considerations of right having been laid aside, all has been staked upon the desire to win the national objective by conquest.

If, for example, keeping to comparatively modern times, we review the principal wars waged by the military autocrats of Europe, we shall find that arbitration, according to any standard of right existing for the time being, and other kindred processes, could have had no application or relation to their real causes. Such monarchs, prompted by ambition and tempted by the apparent relative weakness of others, and possibly in a sense blindly following biological impulses, made war because they wanted it.

It is indeed to be constantly borne in mind, in connexion with the present subject, that among the wars of the past which it would have been difficult to prevent were those which were really due to the desires of ambitious states to try conclusions with other states, and that in the future it may still be difficult to prevent the occasional outbreak of war from similar causes.

It is, of course, the fact that the causes of particular wars have usually been complex in their nature and obscured by the pretensions and arguments of the belligerent states. Nevertheless, for the purposes of practical convenience, the causes of wars in general as between modern civilized peoples may with approximate accuracy be ranged in four classes : (1) Genuine disputes between states as to their mutual rights under the Law of Nations or treaties with regard to particular subject-matters or issues arising between them ; (2) revolts of the spirit of nationality against the position of certain nations or parts of nations within certain states ; (3) changes in the relative strength and territorial or economic requirements of states due to changes in nations ; and (4) ambitious desires on the part of the ruling classes of states or groups of states for enlarged dominions.

Having regard to the considerations indicated in the previous chapter—particularly to the colossal scale on which wars between great states, if waged at all, must henceforth be carried on ; the general disposition of mankind towards peace ; and the practice of resorting to arbitration and other consensual methods of adjusting disputes—it is reasonable to suppose that there is no longer any grave risk of war between the more advanced states from any cause coming within the first of the above classes. But, until the world is much nearer to the time of the general sway of conscience and the prevalence of goodwill than it at present is, it is equally reasonable to apprehend that wars due to causes coming within the other three of these classes will from time to time occur, unless they are prevented by some means which civilization has not hitherto adopted.

The problem is to ascertain how such means may be provided.

PROPOSITION II.—Until the world as a whole

has coalesced into a universal social community, the movements of the spirit of nationality, the natural changes in the relative vigour and population of nations and their economic circumstances, and the desires of ambitious states for enlarged dominion, will, from time to time, cause wars, unless appropriate measures to prevent them are taken collectively by all states or such of them as together possess preponderant power.

CHAPTER III

SOVEREIGNTY

THERE are two outstanding dangers which have to be recognized and avoided by those who are concerned with schemes which are designed for the maintenance of peace. On the one hand there is a prevalent tendency on the part of statesmen and jurists to be unduly hampered by dogmas about Sovereignty. On the other hand there is a readiness on the part of some who have not had the advantage of political experience or legal training to be allured by schemes which involve the creation of an entity which would in reality be a world-state. The term 'super-state,' indeed, which is now in common use, in itself indicates a confusion of ideas as to the nature of a state. The organization which it denotes would not be a state above, or transcending, other states, but would necessarily be the one and only state in existence.

These two dangers may be regarded as the Scylla and Charybdis of the question of peace organization. It will be convenient in this chapter to consider the first.

The juridical nature of sovereignty was expounded by John Austin as follows: 'The superiority which is styled sovereignty, and the independent political society which sovereignty implies, is distinguished from other superiority, and from other society, by the following marks or characters :—1. The *bulk* of the given society are in a *habit* of obedience or submission to a *determinate* and *common* superior : let that common superior be a certain individual person, or a certain body or aggregate of individual persons. 2. That certain individual, or that certain body of individuals, is *not* in a habit of obedience to a determinate human superior. Laws (improperly so called) which opinion sets or imposes, may permanently affect the conduct of that certain individual or body. To express or tacit commands of other determinate parties, that certain individual or body may yield occasional submission. But there is no determinate person, or determinate aggregate of persons, to whose commands, express or tacit, that certain individual or body renders habitual obedience. Or the notions of sovereignty and independent political society may be expressed concisely thus :—If a determinate human superior, not in a habit of obedience to a like superior, receive habitual obedience from the bulk of a given society, that determinate superior is sovereign in that society, and the society (including the superior) is a society political and independent. To that determinate superior, the other members of the society are *subject*. . . . The mutual relation which subsists between that superior and them may be styled *the relation of sovereign and subject*, or *the relation of sovereignty and subjection.*' [1]

The theory thus expounded has been the subject of many weighty criticisms ; but none of these materially lessen the value of the exposition in

[1] *Jurisprudence*, 5th ed. vol. i. pp. 220-1.

connexion with the present subject. This is apparent from the following citations from an essay in which Lord Bryce, after taking such criticisms into account, propounds his own deliberate conclusions upon the subject.

' The term Sovereignty is used in two senses, Legal Supremacy and Practical Mastery. Legal Sovereignty exists in the sphere of Law: it belongs to him who can demand obedience as of Right. Practical Sovereignty exists in the sphere of Fact : it is the power which receives and can by the strong arm enforce obedience. The Legal Sovereign in any State is ascertained by determining the Person (or Body) to whom the law assigns in the last resort the right of issuing general rules or special orders, or of doing acts without incurring liability therefor. The Practical Sovereign is determined by ascertaining who is the Person (or Body) whose will in the last resort prevails (or in case of conflict will be likely to prevail) against all other wills. . . . Practical Sovereignty is, by definition, incapable of being limited (for Law has nothing to do with it), though the exercise of it by its possessor may be restrained by the fear of consequences. . . . Practical Mastery usually ripens, after a certain time, into Legal Authority.' [1]

It is not, of course, to be supposed that the essential elements of sovereignty as thus presented have been consistently present to the minds of those who have made use of the term in modern times, or, indeed, that the word has been by any means uniformly employed with the same meaning,

[1] *Studies in History and Jurisprudence*, vol. ii. pp. 69–72.

or, indeed, with any definite signification whatever.

But from the beginning of the seventeenth
century down to 1919, the word ' sovereignty ' employed in relation to a state had a meaning which
was sufficiently definite to render it a convenient
term for the use of statesmen and writers on International Law. As used by them the words ' a
sovereign state ' meant a political community
which was regarded as being independent of external
control in its foreign relations and which possessed
the right of making war or peace at its own will.
The exercise of this right, moreover, was not merely
the letting loose of armed violence or its subsequent
termination. A war waged by such a state had
certain well recognized juridical consequences.
Being in a certain sense a ' legal ' war it carried
with it the right of the belligerent state to exercise
certain powers against neutrals, including interference with their trade by the institution of
blockades and the seizure of contraband. And a
resulting conquest of territory, when firmly established, had to be recognized. The rights of the
belligerent were in a sense sanctioned by the international customs or morality called International
Law, and the generally received view that the
disregard of such rights would in itself constitute
a *casus belli*.

But no sooner had international law adopted the
conception of a sovereign state than it became
necessary to take cognizance of the existence of
states which, while in themselves political entities,
were not fully independent in the conduct of their
foreign relations. Examples are to be found of

states possessing autonomy as to their internal affairs, accompanied by limitations upon their power of entering into relations with foreign states of the most varied character—ranging from complete exclusion from such relations to limitations little more than formal. It is sufficient to refer as illustrations in this connexion to states subject to a protectorate or suzerainty, colonies under the old system, British India, Neutralized States, the self-governing British Dominions as they were in 1914, and the same Dominions as they are now under the Statute of Westminster.

It may indeed be said that, during the whole of the period in which what is called International Law has been generally recognized, the relations of political communities with one another have become increasingly varied and complicated. Naturally, therefore, from time to time controversies have arisen as to the precise international status to be accorded in particular cases.

But even if the diplomatist or the jurist were able to pronounce definitely in every particular instance whether an existing community is sovereign or not in the classical sense of the word, it is nevertheless the fact that, in the circumstances of the present time, the conception of sovereignty, as a matter of practical politics, is obsolescent, if not extinct. This is, indeed, inferentially recognized in the Covenant of the League of Nations, which, by Article 1, clause 2, provides that ' any fully self-governing State, Dominion, or Colony ' may become a Member of the League.

Moreover, quite apart from the various constitutional or political arrangements which subsist

3

between particular communities, there is to be considered the relation which now subsists between every state, which in any sense forms a political unit and the world-society which has become the recognized foundation of the present international system. The existence of the League of Nations and the treaties by which an unrestricted right of waging war has been generally disclaimed, have indeed tended to render the old conception of a sovereign state an academic abstraction. It should now frankly be recognized that sovereignty, as formerly conceived by statesmen and international jurists, is no longer a characteristic of any state in the modern world.

There is here an extremely significant analogy between the history of Sovereignty and that of the personal independence or liberty of the solitary savage. Each has been transmuted from its original form by social influences and control into something quite different both in its practical and juridical aspects. The external liberty which is now enjoyed by any state is no more than the faculty of doing whatever is not inconsistent with its obligations and duties under the modern system of treaties and international morality. And to limitations which, *mutatis mutandis*, are similar in nature and scope the liberty of the individual in his character as a citizen has long been necessarily subject.

For practical purposes, then, in the modern world-system the unit which has to be considered is the autonomous state. This is the ' person ' with which international politics and peace organizations have now to deal. It may adequately be defined as ' A power exercising jurisdiction over a defined area and not subject to the control of any other individual power.'

In view of the foregoing considerations it would seem that, in weighing the merits of a suggested covenant or arrangement between states, it is no longer a matter of decisive importance that it may be inconsistent with, or a limitation upon, sovereignty as theoretically understood.

PROPOSITION III.—The conception of sovereignty is of little value in connexion with the relations between states in the existing conditions of international life.

CHAPTER IV

THE WORLD-STATE ILLUSION

A N adequate perception of the causes which may still lead to wars will enable us to appreciate the difficulty of the great problem as to the best means of establishing a durable peace which now confronts statesmen and jurists, and indeed all men of intelligence and goodwill.

In order that effective means of counteracting these causes may be ascertained, it is important that the principal categories of plausible suggestions which are likely to divert attention from the real points for consideration and to lead inquirers in wrong directions should be critically examined. When we realize that schemes which to many appear to be obvious ways of avoiding wars are at present impracticable, and that it is certain that for many generations to come they must remain only ideals, we shall be the more likely to concentrate our attention upon appropriate measures.

Many thinkers both in former ages and in our own time have advanced what may conveniently be termed a juristic solution of the problem. They have boldly contended that in the society of states order must be established and maintained substantially in the same way as it has already been established and is now maintained in the case of societies of individuals. The communities which we call states must in their view be rendered subject to a universal law enforced by a competent authority which must be supported by an adequate force. Some have put the suggestion in a strictly logical form, and have contemplated avowedly a *civitas maxima*—a world-state—from which *ex hypothesi* interstatal wars would be excluded.

Now, in the first place, it is to be observed that few, if any, states, and certainly none of the Great Powers, would be willing to take part in the formation of such a state. But, even if it were otherwise and there were a general disposition to co-operate in this direction, it would still be quite impracticable to create a world-state which would be a stable or permanent reality, or a central government which would be adequately efficient and influential.

A state may comprise several nations ; and a large proportion of its population may be alien from the governing race or races. But, although a state is in a sense an artificial entity, it cannot endure for any lengthened period, unless it is supported by the operation of natural causes among its citizens. Its cohesion is dependent upon community of sentiment and interest on the part of its people, or at least of a predominant section of them. This community generally depends upon some or all of the usual features of a common nationality— common blood, language, religion, customs, and traditions. In some stages of society it may mainly depend upon a common interest in combining for the purposes of defence against external enemies ; and even at the present time this kind of interest is still potent in binding together the constituent communities of great political unions. Without, however, some such strong and enduring basis of common feeling, no aggregate of individuals could evolve and maintain a government capable of exercising effective control over their conduct and strong enough to overwhelm any opposition to its authority. They could not establish the conditions necessary to the maintenance of general order. They could not avert that speedy dissolution of their collective existence which would be the inevitable consequence of its want of the essential elements of social cohesion.

In order that a world-state should attain a condition of stable equilibrium, it would be necessary that the constituent communities generally should be satisfied with the governmental structure and that the governing body should be capable of exercising a restraining authority throughout every quarter of the globe. Neither of these conditions could exist without a far greater community of sympathy and sense of homogeneity and brotherhood than now exist between the various peoples of the world. Loyalty to the human race as a whole is still lukewarm in almost all hearts as compared with loyalty to the nation and the state. Centuries of closer intercourse and broader education must pass away before the divers nations will have sufficient mental and moral affinity with one another to render practicable their coalescence into a great community with a collective civil life. Meanwhile the negative interest in the prevention of war, even

if, for the time being, it furnished a sufficient motive
for the constitution of a united state, would tend
to diminish in strength as the period of peace
lengthened and the horrors of war receded into the
distance of the past. A nominal political unity
would not prevent dissension. Nor would the
armed strife of nations be any the less odious than
before because lawyers might choose to describe
it as rebellion or civil war.

Moreover, any general and serious attempt to
establish a world-state, although it would be impotent to create the desired new organization,
would tend towards the destruction of the systems
already in existence. Instead of creating a world-
community it would weaken the cohesion of the
larger social aggregates which have been developed
by the labours and sacrifices of past ages.

Probably, however, the suggestion of a world-
state in its crude form will not attract the support of any very considerable proportion of those
who are interested in the subject of organization
for peace. The danger in this connexion lies rather
in the possibility of a confusion of thought with
regard to schemes which, under some other name,
are really open to objections similar to those which
have been briefly indicated to the suggestion of a
world-state as ordinarily understood. This is
particularly the case with regard to the detailed
provisions sometimes urged in connexion with
the proposal which has often been made that International Law should be upheld throughout the
world by a Force charged with the function of
restraining or punishing breaches of its provisions.
The distinctions which have to be borne in mind

in regard to such schemes are dealt with in Chapter VI.

PROPOSITION IV.—In the existing condition of mankind, the establishment of a world-state is not practicable.

CHAPTER V

CONFEDERATION

THE general opinion of those who are interested in either the theoretical or practical consideration of world-organization for the maintenance of peace is at the present time clearly favourable to the kind of union which German writers call a Zweckerband [1]—a union of states primarily for the particular purpose of securing peace, and which, apart from the measures and conditions involved in the furtherance of this common purpose, leaves each state all the autonomy which is consistent therewith.

It is accordingly important that the juridical nature of such a union should be precisely appreciated.

Federation may mean a union of one or other of two radically different kinds. In the proper and more usual sense of the word it means a combination of several states into one, the supreme authority in which is shared by a central government with the governments of the communities which have become united together. The federated states irrevocably cease to be respectively separate political communities. Thenceforth they are constituent parts of one state, to the central government of which is confided the conduct of

[1] Cf. *War, Peace, and the Future*, by Ellen Key, pp. 121-2.

their external relations. The union of the North
American Colonies, which became the United States
of America, was a federation of this character.
In the other sense of the word, federation means
a treaty of alliance for a particular object or objects
which is intended to be permanent ; as the result
of which the contracting states, while severally
retaining their separate political existence, are
thenceforth regarded as a permanent confederacy
of states.

This distinction between the two meanings of the
word ' federation ' corresponds to that which is
drawn by Austin in the following passage between
a ' composite state ' and a ' system of confederated
states.'

' In the case of a *composite state*, the several
united societies are one independent society, or
are severally subject to one sovereign body, which,
through its minister the general government,
and through its members and ministers the several
united governments, is habitually and generally
obeyed in each of the united societies, and also
in the larger society arising from the union of all.
In the case of a *system of confederated states*, the
several compacted societies are not one society,
and are not subject to a common sovereign ; or
(changing the phrase) each of the several societies
is an independent political society, and each of
their several governments is properly sovereign or
supreme. Though the aggregate of the several
governments was the framer of the federal compact,
and may subsequently pass resolutions concerning
the entire confederacy, neither the terms of that
compact nor such subsequent resolutions are

enforced in any of the societies by the authority of that aggregate body. To each of the confederated governments, those terms and resolutions are merely articles of agreement which it spontaneously adopts ; and they owe their legal effect, in its own political society, to laws and other commands which it makes or fashions upon them, and which, of its own authority, it addresses to its own subjects. In short, a system of confederated states is not essentially different from a number of independent governments connected by an ordinary alliance. And where independent governments are connected by an ordinary alliance, none of the allied governments is subject to the allied governments considered as an aggregate body : though each of the allied governments adopts the terms of the alliance, and commonly enforces those terms, by laws and commands of its own, in its own independent community. Indeed, a system of confederated states, and a number of independent governments connected by an ordinary alliance, cannot be distinguished precisely through general or abstract expressions. So long as we abide in general expressions, we can only affirm, generally and vaguely, that the compact of the former is intended to be permanent, whilst the alliance of the latter is commonly intended to be temporary ; and that the ends or purposes which are embraced by the compact are commonly more numerous, and are commonly more complicated, than those which the alliance contemplates.' [1]

There is thus an essential distinction which it is necessary for the present purpose to keep con-

[1] Austin's *Jurisprudence*, 5th ed. vol. i. pp. 261–2.

stantly in mind. Federation in the one sense involves the creation of a central government empowered to enforce the sovereign will of the entire community against any particular constituent part, and also the absence of any right on the part of the constituent communities to withdraw from the composite state. Federation in the other sense does not involve the creation of any such central government ; it leaves the confederated states in point of autonomy in the same position as they occupied before. Apart from moral and other incidental effects, its essential result in this case is merely that each of the several allied states is bound by its agreement to a certain course of conduct.

Federation, in the first of the foregoing meanings, applied to the society of states as a whole, would obviously involve the creation of a world-state, which we have seen is, for the time being, impracticable. And it is this kind of union which is really involved in many of the schemes in which federation has been proposed as a means of maintaining peace ; although, generally speaking, the authors of these schemes do not appear to have appreciated this fact. Certainly they do not, for the most part, seem to have contemplated the obliteration of the international personality of the several states which the formation of a world-state would involve.

As an instance of proposals of federation in the other meaning of the word, reference may be made to the following passages in Kant's essay on *Perpetual Peace*.

His ' Second Definitive Article of Perpetual Peace '

is : ' The law of nations shall be founded on a federation of free states.' ' Every state,' he says, ' for the sake of its own security, may—and ought to—demand that its neighbour should submit itself to conditions similar to those of the civil society where the right of every individual is guaranteed. This would give rise to a federation of nations which, however, would not have to be a state of nations. That would involve a contradiction. For the term " state " implies the relation of one who rules to those who obey—that is to say, of lawgiver to the subject people ; and many nations in one state would constitute only one nation, which contradicts our hypothesis, since here we have to consider the right of one nation against another, in so far as they are so many separate states and are not to be fused into one.' [1] ' Instead of the positive idea of a world-republic, if all is not to be lost, only the negative substitute for it, a federation averting war, maintaining its ground, and ever extending over the world, may stop the current of this tendency to war and shrinking from the control of law. But even then there will be a constant danger that this propensity may break out.' [2] And, in an appendix to the essay, he says : ' We have seen above that something of the nature of a federation between nations, for the sole purpose of doing away with war, is the only rightful condition of things reconcilable with their individual freedom.' [3]

Now, in regard to a federation of the kind thus

[1] *Perpetual Peace*, translated by Miss M. Campbell Smith, pp. 128, 129.
[2] *Ibid.* p. 136.　　　　　[3] *Ibid.* pp. 192-3.

proposed by Kant, it is to be observed that it leaves the measures to be taken for the prevention of war to the several separate states acting in accordance with their obligations under the treaty which has been entered into between them. Such a federation has been realized in the League of Nations.

In reviewing any suggested scheme for the further development of this organization, it will be convenient to examine it in the light of the distinction which has thus been indicated. If, and in so far as, the scheme involves the creation of a world-state, it is, for the present, impracticable. On the other hand, if it does not involve this, its real scope is somewhat obscured by the use of the word ' federation.' Its strength will depend upon the degree in which it is calculated to bring about a sufficient solidarity of opinion and co-operation in active measures on the part of the several states concerned to prevent or terminate any breaches of the peace.

PROPOSITION V.—For the time being peace can be forcibly maintained only by means of the co-operation of states as separate political entities.

CHAPTER VI

AN INTERNATIONAL FORCE

MANY people who do not contemplate the creation of a world-state as a measure of practical politics, nevertheless advocate the establishment of a world-force to the exclusion of the forces of individual states. In weighing proposals made with this object, exceptionally careful discrimination is necessary. The question involved really becomes mainly one of degree.

An International Force may mean a Collective Force composed of contingents provided by the Great Powers (and perhaps some other states), respectively mobilized in pursuance of definite undertakings embodied in a treaty intended to be permanent in character. The existence and employment of this Force would involve the co-operation of the covenanting Powers. Co-operation involves the existence of separate entities set in motion by separate wills or controlling authorities. Such a force would accordingly be consistent with the continued existence of separate states and with the stage of social integration at which the world has already arrived. It does not postulate a condition of world unity which in fact has not yet been attained. The proposal to establish this Force is eminently practicable, as is hereafter shown in Chapter XIX.

On the other hand, many writers have urged the establishment of an International Force, in the sense of a Supreme Executive Force, so constituted and controlled as to be fundamentally inconsistent with the interstatal order which now exists and which must for a long time to come still continue necessary. It may be true that, in order to make adequate provision for the general security and peace, it is necessary to go far in the direction so proposed. And it is also probably true that such proposals appear superficially very similar to those for a Collective Force which are hereafter considered. There is, however, in reality a distinction which is of decisive importance. Whereas the Collective Force postulates the co-operation of separate states, a Supreme Executive Force involves the unified dominion of one central authority to the exclusion of all others.

A world-state, a law universally obligatory, and a Supreme Executive Force, are severally aspects of one and the same political constitution. Each of the three conceptions really involves the other two. Each of these, moreover, if realized, would involve the sacrifice of that autonomy which is essential to the existence of the states which now compose the world society. In other words, a universally operative force, not arbitrary or un-regulated, or dependent upon the voluntary, though covenanted, co-operation of the several Powers, but immediately and permanently at the disposal, and subject to the direct control, of a central council, would exclude autonomy and separate statal existence on the part of any members of the community in which it prevailed.

A Supreme Executive Force, *ex vi termini*, would be capable of coercing any of the Powers which had been parties to its constitution. Its existence would involve its control by a central council authorized to issue mandates and to enforce compliance therewith by directing the Force against any community or individuals which should disregard them. A universal habit of obedience to this council would necessarily develop. On the other hand, the council would not be under the necessity of deferring to any authority outside its own. It would thus be the sovereign body of the entire world. It alone would be independent ; all other bodies and persons would be dependent upon it. The law which it enforced would not be international or interstatal. It would be the law of the one and only world-state formed by the united communities which, upon assenting to the constitution of the Supreme Executive Force, had ceased to be separate political entities.

In short, a coercive power compelling obedience to the decrees of the body by which it was directly wielded and to the system of law which it applied, would involve the exclusive sovereignty of this body and the operation of the law over all who were subject to its power. A Supreme Executive Force would involve the establishment of a world-state and the cessation of the existence of all other states.

We ought, however, to bear in mind that, although Sovereignty, Law, and Independence are the objects of definite conceptions, they are not in fact absolutely realized in human affairs. They are, indeed, essentially matters of degree. It is generally

4

possible to decide with confidence whether or not a particular community is a state or a certain general proposition is a law ; but in some cases it is otherwise. And new adjustments of interstatal relations, involving developments in the direction of a common sovereignty, or a universal law, may well become desirable in the near future. It is sufficient here to urge that, for the time being, an attempt to approach so closely to the constitution of a world-state as to render the power of a central council more conspicuous and certain than the freedom of action of the Great Powers respectively, would be more likely to prove disastrous than beneficial. So long, however, as it is recognized that the conception of a world-state, or even of a Supreme Executive Force, for the purpose of upholding a universally obligatory system of law, cannot for the present be realized by direct means, the idea itself may be useful as suggesting schemes which may be established immediately, or as presenting to the mind a far distant objective, the contemplation of which may help us to move onward in the right direction.

PROPOSITION VI.—No method of preserving peace which would involve the existence of a common and plenary sovereignty over the Great Powers is at present practicable.

CHAPTER VII

THE FOUNDATIONS OF PEACE

WITHIN the borders of every civilized community order is for the most part maintained. Any tendencies on the part of the citizens to crime, anarchy, or civil war are restrained within comparatively narrow limits. But the world has yet to establish permanent order between civilized communities themselves.

We have seen that it is not practicable to secure a lasting peace by setting up in the society of states the machinery of sovereignty and positive law. Accordingly, there is in reality no simple and obvious means of ensuring the attainment of the desired object. The recognition of this negative truth is of the greatest practical importance. Without it one can hardly be in a position to appreciate the gravity of the difficulties which beset the problem before us or likely to discover its solution. On the other hand, when once we have appreciated the position as it really is, we shall see that it calls for patient and laborious study as well as for the motive power of ardent enthusiasm.

Beginning, then, as it were, *de novo*, we must carefully inquire into each and all of the means which are, or may be, available for the purpose of preventing wars.

States are great corporations of which the

members are human beings. Accordingly, the action of states is determined by motives which are either the same as, or analogous to, those which determine the conduct of individual men. In order, therefore, to ascertain fully ' the things which make for peace ' between states, we must in the first place review the means whereby the conduct of individuals is guided and controlled.

We must at the outset distinguish between influences which operate in the formation of character and influences which directly regulate conduct. It is clear that everything which tends to establish in any one a good disposition—to quicken conscience and to develop a virtuous character—is indirectly of paramount importance in relation to his conduct. Everything which tends to make an individual good must tend also to cause his conduct to be right. Accordingly, all that is comprised in education in the most comprehensive sense, and especially the general tone of the community in which the citizen is reared, indirectly affect his conduct. The ultimate desideratum, indeed, is that men should be brought into such a moral condition that they would do right habitually and without difficulty or even conscious effort.

By the elevation of individuals the nations and states to which they belong are themselves elevated. Everything which improves the moral character of the citizens tends to produce the righteousness which ' exalteth a nation ' and to increase the probability that the actions of their government will be right. In a state the citizens of which were good men the ruling powers would not be likely to wage a war which was manifestly unjust.   Accordingly, we ought to recognize fully and clearly the supremely important truth that every one who, in any part of the world and by any means whatever, is working for the moral advancement of mankind, is at the same time promoting goodwill among the nations and the cause of peace throughout the society of states.   The good disposition is a peaceable disposition, and is, as it were, the main element in the foundations of permanent peace.

Spiritual and temporal welfare are also among the conditions which predispose mankind to peace. Other things being equal, a happy and contented being is less prone to stir up strife than one whose life is passed in an attitude of revolt against his own environment.   And so the disposition of the citizens of a particular community towards the *status quo* of their corporate existence has an important bearing upon the external influence of their state. A community which is dissatisfied and restless, or which is frequently or for any long period torn by internal dissensions, is apt to be the cause of disturbance of the peace outside its own borders.

In order that the citizens of a particular state may be in a condition of contentment and orderly stability, the state must fulfil its true function as the organ of the corporate unity of the people, whereby they are enabled to realize fully their social and collective life.   The spirit of nationality must breathe freely within the political structure of the community, and the system of government must be acceptable to the citizens at large.

If part of a nation comprised within one state desire political union with the rest of their race

who are in allegiance with another, there will be
a tendency to instability in the relations of the two
states immediately concerned which may result in
a disturbance of the equilibrium of the society of
states itself. So, if a nation, or part of a nation,
feel oppressed by the domination of another race,
or for any other reason feel that their national
life is out of harmony with their political position
and are anxious to escape from their civic allegiance,
a similar disturbance will be probable. Civil war
may easily lead to international complications.
War indeed in any form is a fiery evil which tends
to spread so long as it remains unextinguished.

Wherever, therefore, the spirit of nationality is
in revolt against the existing political order the
disposition for peace must be imperfect. It is
accordingly pre-eminently important that, in the
settlements of territorial boundaries, whenever the
opportunity offers, regard should be paid to nationality so far as it is a potent reality. Public right can
obtain full and lasting recognition only upon the
condition of its substantial correspondence with the
real sentiments of the living nations.

The form of the government of a state has moreover
an important bearing upon its external influence,
apart from the question of the general acquiescence
of the citizens in its existence.

Self-respect and a sense of responsibility on the
part of an individual are among the best securities
for the goodness of his intentions ; while a habit of
rational reflection upon questions of difficulty and
importance affords the most reliable ground for
confidence in the wisdom of his actions. In a state
where representative government prevails there is

the amplest scope for the development in the citizens both individually and collectively of an enlightened and comprehensive respect both for themselves and for their country. The sense of responsibility also for the actions of their government in relation to other states must almost inevitably exist in more or less amplitude and vigour throughout the electorate. The people as a whole, moreover, naturally take an intelligent and sustained interest in the public affairs of their state ; they become accustomed to weigh disputed questions according to the standards of justice and expediency ; and they acquire the habit of acquiescing in the decision of disputed issues according to the reason and conscience of majorities. The executive government itself is responsible to them and must carry their approval with it whenever it embarks upon a course of action of grave importance to the community. The necessity for this approval is a check upon foolish and unrighteous wars, the efficacy and value of which must of course largely depend upon the intelligence and integrity of the people at large. In the case, however, of a democratic state the danger of the personal ambitions or idiosyncrasies of individuals involving the community in hostilities must necessarily be considerably less than that which exists in the case of empires and kingdoms which are governed autocratically. Accordingly, there is solid ground for believing that the extension of representative institutions will on the whole be favourable to the cause of peace.

A good disposition leads to results of practical beneficence in proportion to the scope of the sympathies by which its activities are directed. Sym-

pathy is evoked by social intercourse. Even the
most casual conversation between strangers generally
disposes both to reciprocal civility. The social instincts of the race have in fact long been dominant
among civilized men. Friendship necessarily tends
to exclude strife. But it is of practical importance
to realize also that the mere fact of acquaintance
resulting from social intercourse of any kind in
itself generally has the effect of disposing men to
mutual consideration and goodwill.

Everything, therefore, which tends to the development of a sympathetic attitude on the part of the
citizens of the several states towards those of others
will contribute to the establishment of lasting peace.
The various agencies whereby the different peoples
are brought into communication with one another
will in their several ways tend to the promotion of
general goodwill. Especially will this be the case
in so far as common interests are developed. Conferences of workmen, savants, artists, or others,
from divers countries, will in effect generally be
peace conferences. Even purely business relations,
though susceptible of misuse, will in the main have
a tendency in the right direction ; for the trader has
usually a sympathetic interest in the well-being and
prosperity of his customers.

The operative effect of the various means of
laying the foundations for the establishment of the
conditions favourable to the maintenance of
general peace, which we have thus briefly indicated,
must necessarily be realized only gradually. We
cannot reasonably expect that these means by
themselves will be adequate for the prevention of
war until many future generations of men shall

have passed away from the earth. Meanwhile the preservation of peace is the most pressing of all the needs of mankind. Accordingly, it is not sufficient for our purpose to recognize and observe the principles and methods prescribed by reason for the promotion of the moral health and social welfare of the various nations and states. We must at the same time endeavour to discover and apply specific remedies for the occasional tendency to strife to which they are still subject and which is in itself in the nature of a dangerous disorder of their systems.

With a view, therefore, to the attainment of the best possible results in the immediate future, we must concentrate our attention upon the external influences by which, in the world as it now is, conduct may be regulated directly.

PROPOSITION VII.—States will be inclined to a peaceable disposition by the moral elevation of their citizens ; the correspondence of national sentiment with political allegiance ; the existence of representative government ; and the prevalence of social relations between the various peoples.

CHAPTER VIII

THE REGULATION OF CONDUCT

WITH the object of ascertaining the means which are available for the control of the conduct of states, we must now review the various ways in which the conduct of individual men is regulated.

Human beings in general are restrained from wrongful aggression upon their neighbours, and constrained to action necessary for the collective welfare of the society to which they belong, by the operation upon their minds of certain forces or influences which may be distinguished as follows : (1) Extraneous Physical Force ; (2) Administrative (or Arbitrary) Authority ; (3) Sacerdotal Authority ; (4) Custom ; (5) Convention ; (6) Positive Law ; (7) the Social Imperative ; and (8) Public Opinion.

Whenever an individual, not wholly in deference to his own conscience, refrains from doing anything to which his immediate view of his interest, or his passion, inclines him ; or does that from which, owing to the operation of similar motives, he feels averse, or which he would not do merely for the purpose of gratifying any immediate selfish desire on his own part, it is to one or more of these forces or influences that he defers.

Throughout the historical period all these sources of authority have to a greater or less extent prevailed among men and have assisted the race in its general moral development ; but their relative importance has varied from time to time.   Hitherto it would seem that they have all been, as it were, necessary concomitants of the social organizations of mankind, and as yet there is no immediate prospect that any of them will cease to be operative. Accordingly, it will be convenient for the purpose of this treatise to define them severally, and then to proceed to the consideration of their practical bearing upon the problem in hand.

EXTRANEOUS FORCE

Every man is influenced by the existence of the physical force residing in other people.   This influence operates independently of the existence of any relationship to which authority or the right of control is attached by law or custom or otherwise, or any reciprocal obligations arising out of common membership of a particular community. It operates as between all men who come into contact with one another, irrespectively of the time or place or other circumstances of the case.

The demeanour of the rudest savage on meeting other people, whether members of his own tribe or not, would, generally speaking, be regulated to a certain extent by his view of their efficiency as compared with his own in a possible combat.   However fierce in disposition and prone to violence he might be, he would be slow to indulge in wanton and open aggression upon a party obviously superior to himself in fighting strength.   Less crudely and directly, but none the less certainly, the most valiant and polite gentleman in Christendom is influenced by the physical power of others. It constitutes a standing warning against exploits of a quixotic character. The conduct of a sane man, indeed, so long as he is not absolutely deprived of good sense by anger, will always be qualified and limited by a perception of the futility of attempting the impossible, and the undesirability of provoking a contest in which his own defeat would be certain. At the same time, it is of course true that, while the savage and the criminal find in their appreciation of the force possessed by others a restraint upon cruel or predatory instincts which operates upon their minds directly, the well-disposed citizen, although habitually influenced by the fact of the existence of this force, does not, generally speaking, consciously advert to it.

Accordingly, in the rudest society some sort of temporary equilibrium is from time to time obtained by virtue of the general recognition of this force. And in the most advanced civilization conduct is still regulated—manners are softened and provocative demeanour is prevented—by its ever present though usually quiescent power.

ADMINISTRATIVE AUTHORITY

Administrative authority, in this connexion, means the authority exercised by a superior over an inferior in so far as it is not limited to the mere enforcement of a pre-existing general rule. It is the discretionary control exercised by one person over another as between whom and himself there exists a definite relation of superiority and inferiority.   The power of issuing commands supported by a sufficient sanction (or prospective punishment in case of disobedience) resides in a person or body, legally or practically recognized as a constituted authority by the person who is subject thereto.   The exercise of this power is arbitrary in the sense that it consists of particular commands of which the provisions are dependent, within the limits, if any, of the scope of the authority, upon the discretion of those by whom they are issued.

In this category a vast area of human relations is comprised.   It ranges from parental authority to the autocracy of an absolute monarch.   It includes the power of the chieftain of a savage tribe as well as the supreme authority of a democratic state. It also includes all discretionary authority residing in persons who are themselves subject to the law of their land or responsible to an authority higher than their own.   It therefore comprises the more salient and pervading aspects of the authority exercised even in republics and constitutional states, within the limits allowed to their discretion, by preceptors, masters, managers, naval and military officers, skippers, prison officials and the like, as well as the authority exercised by persons or bodies acting in pursuance of powers of local or departmental government.

The point of importance in this connexion is the large part which is taken by central and local administrative authorities in the affairs of all settled communities.

The existence of a state involves on the part of the government not only the adoption or enactment of laws or general rules of conduct (which will be considered hereafter) and their enforcement, but also the issue and enforcement of occasional or particular commands, by which specific acts or forbearances are required from some or all of its citizens. General rules are the means by which the conduct of human beings is regulated so far as acts or forbearances of any predetermined class are required at their hands. But the people who collectively constitute the natural substratum of the state, whether considered individually or together, are living organisms, and as such their mutual relations and their needs are continually changing. These dynamic conditions give rise to the necessity for governmental ordinances *ad hoc*. It is impracticable to govern satisfactorily any community by general rules alone. Exigencies due to the actions and reactions of the living social organism upon its environment and which cannot be subsumed to general rules are continually recurring. In such cases the collective will—the will of the governing authority—must be exercised in administrative action.

Accordingly, the social life of a community cannot be carried on in reliance merely upon laws, police, judges, sheriffs, and prisons. The commands or particular orders of governors or governing bodies are as necessary as the laws established by custom or the legislature. Ministers are as essential to the commonwealth as judges. Administration is as necessary as a system of judicature. All this indeed is implied by the very word *government*.

Broadly speaking, it may be said that, as civilization advances and the conditions of the national life become more settled, the greater are the number of categories of the civic life which can be subjected to general rules and the wider accordingly is the area in which general rules prevail. Moreover, a good constitution will provide suitable means for the restraint of those who exercise administrative power from its abuse. But the fact remains that, concurrently with the reign of law, there exists the necessity for the edicts of administrative authority. Some persons or bodies must govern. Power which is arbitrary in the sense of not being restricted in its exercise to the application of a rule to certain facts—power which within limits, however narrow, can be exercised according to a discretionary choice—is essential to human society in its present state. So long as any government whatever is necessary, there will always be some scope—however restricted —for purely administrative orders.

The tripartite distribution of supreme powers into (1) Legislative, (2) Administrative, and (3) Executive, although its essential accuracy should be obvious, is, as a matter of fact, very generally overlooked by both jurists and laymen in this country. It is important to appreciate the reasons for this.

In Britain and other parts of the world mainly peopled by men of British descent, owing to the facts that for a long time internal order has been prevalent and the reign of law fully established, the area of arbitrary or discretionary authority, other than that of the supreme legislature, has been reduced within certain definite limits. The citizens have for generations enjoyed the right of testing the validity of almost any act of an administrative authority affecting their own interests by instituting proceedings in the ordinary courts of justice. Thus the action of the central government, as well as that of local administrative authorities, has been restrained by the application of general provisions of the law. So far indeed has this process tended to exclude from official action any appearance of oppression that, under the conditions prevalent in times of peace and apart from any sudden and grave emergency, an adult civilian hardly recognizes the true character of the administrative orders with which he is obliged to comply, except, perhaps, in matters of comparatively trivial importance.

The real activity of administrative authority in Great Britain is moreover to a large extent obscured by the powers and methods of the Imperial Parliament. This body is not only the legislature but the supreme administrative authority as well. It can in fact do whatever it pleases. So long as it observes the forms prescribed for the time being for its own enactments, it is completely free from legal restraints. When it arrives at a determination, and expresses its will according to those forms, it enacts a statute of the realm. It is not surprising that people do not distinguish between the nature of one statute and that of another. In current phraseology whatever Parliament enacts is the law of the land. In the widest meaning, however, in which the word ' law ' has any definite relation to conduct it always signifies a general rule. And if we examine any volume of the statutes we shall discover that the bulk of the contents does not consist of enactments which are wholly of the nature of laws but of statutes which either wholly or partly are of the nature of occasional or particular commands. Acts of Parliament, indeed, are very largely a form of administration—the means by which, on the motion of administrative officials, the will of the community is applied to the needs for the time being of the commonwealth as a living and ever-changing organism. They are ordinances which are requisite in the interests of the state so far as these cannot be defined in standing propositions of a generic character.

The co-ordinate and equal importance of administration in relation to law is further manifest when we survey the various offices of state and the local governing authorities. If society required only laws or general rules and an executive to enforce them, there would be comparatively little reason for the existence of most of the ministries or departments of government, and the vast number of local bodies which are engaged in administrative work. It is true that, in the form of by-laws and other regulations, these authorities frame orders which consist of general rules and are therefore laws ; but the making of such regulations is by no means the main part of their business. Even if we exclude from our consideration in this connexion the departments concerned with the foreign relations of the Empire, or with its defence or fiscal necessities, we shall find that the work of other ministries, for example the Ministry of Health, the Boards of Trade, Education, and Agriculture, as well as that of the county, borough, and other local authorities, is mainly concerned with administration. No ordinance of any of these bodies may contravene the provisions of the law. But this qualification does not in any way exclude

5

the exercise of discretion within the prescribed limits, or prevent such an ordinance from being in its nature a particular command or act of administration.

What has been said of a state applies *mutatis mutandis* to any society. The governing body or person, through whom the collective will or authority is declared or exercised—whether the council of a college, the board of directors of a trading company, the committee of a club, or the head of a family—must formulate and uphold general rules. But the needs of the society will render it also imperative that administrative orders—occasional commands adapted to special states of fact—should also from time to time be issued.

We shall hereafter see that the distinction which we have thus endeavoured to enforce lies at the very root of the momentous problem with which this treatise is concerned.

SACERDOTAL AUTHORITY

Where a man shapes his conduct in a particular way in deference to what he is informed by a fellow-creature is the will of a supernatural being he yields to an authority which may be called sacerdotal.

This kind of authority differs from administrative authority, as described above, in so far as obedience thereto is constrained by the belief in the supernatural sanction and not by the power actually residing in the functionary who professes to declare the supernatural will. Similarly it differs from the authority of conscience and of religion (in the more usual meaning of this word at the present time) in so far as obedience is yielded by reason of the fear of its sanction and not simply because of the belief in the righteousness of the particular course of action which is directed.   It is, however, obvious that, although in essential characteristics these kinds of authority or influences are quite distinct, there is in fact much intermingling of them in practice.

The word ' sacerdotal ' is adopted in this connexion as the most convenient for the purpose. But it will be remembered that the king or chieftain was in early times himself the priest.   Moreover, authority which is essentially of the character of that now under consideration has often been and still is exercised by individuals not invested with either the royal or the priestly character.

' The earliest notions,' says Sir Henry Maine,[1] ' connected with the conception, now so fully developed, of a law or rule of life, are those contained in the Homeric words " Themis " and " Themistes." . . . When a king decided a dispute by a sentence, the judgment was assumed to be the result of direct inspiration.   The divine agent, suggesting judicial awards to kings or to gods, the greatest of kings, was *Themis*. . . . Themistes . . . are the awards themselves divinely dictated to the   judge. . . . They are separate, isolated judgments.'

Similarly, Spencer says : [2] ' There come methods by which the will of the ancestor, or the dead chief, or the derived deity, is sought ; and the reply given, usually referring to a particular occasion, originates in some cases a precedent, from which there results a law.'

In the Roman state, to refer to one leading

---

[1] *Ancient Law* (Sir F. Pollock's (1930) ed.), pp. 3, 4.
[2] *Principles of Sociology*, vol. ii. p. 515.

illustration, this authority was long habitually exercised by the college of augurs. The tendency to seek for oracular utterances and to defer to them has indeed been a very general incident of human nature in the past.

The kind of authority now under consideration is still exercised throughout the largest ecclesiastical organizations in Christendom, as well as to some extent in other religious communities. No doubt there are many people who are entirely free from its influence, or at least believe that they are. On the other hand, there are probably many who defer to this authority without recognizing its true character.

Custom

Whenever any one acts, or forbears from acting, in a certain way because he wishes to comply with a usage established among the people with whom he is living, he defers to the authority of custom. In so far as he exercises a conscious election in the matter, he is influenced by the desire to avoid the disapproval of his fellows, which he apprehends would ensue upon a departure from the course prescribed by general usage.

Custom differs from the foregoing kinds of authority inasmuch as it enforces a general rule of conduct, as distinguished from a particular or occasional command. It differs from law in the nature of its sanction : it is not enforced by a definitely prescribed penalty imposed by a determinate human superior. There is room for vagueness and uncertainty, both as to the character of the evil consequences, if any, which will follow upon disobedience to the rule, and also as to the persons by whom they will be inflicted. Where the sanction becomes definite and the person or body at whose hands it will be suffered becomes determinate, the rule of custom is transmuted into a rule of law. This change is effected whenever a custom is recognized and enforced by the tribunals of a state.

The propensity to evolve, and afterwards follow, customs is universal; and human life cannot be imagined as subsisting in complete independence of this kind of authority. It is traceable wherever any record of society exists. Indeed, it would be difficult to say whether the ignorant savage or the civilized citizen is the more thoroughly under its control.

The growth of custom is thus explained by Professor Holland: [1] ' Its chief characteristic is that it is a generally observed course of conduct. No one was ever consciously present at the commencement of such a course of conduct, but we can hardly doubt that it originated generally in the conscious choice of the more convenient of two acts, though sometimes doubtless in the accidental adoption of one of two indifferent alternatives; the choice in either case having been either deliberately or accidentally repeated till it ripened into habit. The best illustration of the formation of such habitual courses of action is the mode in which a path is formed across a common. One man crosses the common, in the direction which is suggested either by the purpose he has in view, or by mere accident. If others follow in the same track, which they are likely to do after it has once been trodden, a path is made. Before a custom is formed there is no juristic reason

[1] *Jurisprudence*, 13th ed. pp. 57-8.

for its taking one direction rather than another, though doubtless there was some ground of expediency, of religious scruple, or of accidental suggestion. A habitual course of action once formed gathers strength and sanctity every year. It is a course of action which every one is accustomed to see followed : it is generally believed to be salutary, and any deviation from it is felt to be abnormal, immoral. It has never been enjoined by the organized authority of the state, but it has been unquestioningly obeyed by the individuals of which the state is composed. There can in fact be no doubt that customary rules existed among peoples long before nations or states had come into being.'

Convention

Whenever a man acts, or forbears from acting, in a certain way because he conceives that he is bound to such action or forbearance by virtue of an agreement, express or implied, to which he has been a party, he defers to the authority of convention.

Agreements are for the most part upheld by one or more of the other kinds of authority which are now under review, and it may accordingly be contended with much force that convention is not in itself an independent category of authority.

Apparently, however, human nature, even in its rudest form, perceives some constraining influence —some independent source of authority—in an agreement as such. ' Pactum serva ' has been felt to be an obligatory principle, not only by the citizens of highly civilized states, but generally speaking by all good people throughout historic times. The evolution of order has in fact been largely due to agreements. Grotius, indeed, says : ' Since it is conformable to Natural Law to observe compacts (for some mode of obliging themselves was necessary among men and no other natural mode could be imagined) Civil Rights were derived from this source, mutual compact.' [1]

The very fact of the making of an agreement involves the assumption that an accepted promise is the basis of an obligation. ' This obligation depends upon the expectations which we knowingly and voluntarily excite.' [2] The man who could make an agreement without any appreciation whatever of a consequent *primâ facie* reason for keeping it would be morally insane.

It is accordingly not only convenient but probably not altogether unsound logically to treat convention in the way here adopted.

POSITIVE LAW

When a man acts, or refrains from acting, in a certain way in obedience to a rule, compliance with which is enforceable by functionaries whose proceedings are in the last resort supported by the supreme central authority of the community of which he is a member (or to which for the time being he owes allegiance), he defers to the authority of positive law.

' Every positive law, or every law simply and strictly so called,' says John Austin, ' is set by a sovereign person, or a sovereign body of persons,

---

[1] *De Jure Belli et Pacis*, Prolegomena 15 (Whewell's translation).
[2] Paley's *Moral Philosophy*, bk. iii. pt. i. ch. v. ii.

to a member or members of the independent political society wherein that person or body is sovereign or supreme. Or (changing the expression) it is set by a monarch, or sovereign number, to a person or persons in a state of subjection to its author. Even though it sprung directly from another fountain or source, it *is* a positive law, or a law strictly so called, by the institution of that present sovereign in the character of political superior.' [1]

The word ' law ' is used with divers meanings. But it is convenient that, when the regulation of human conduct is dealt with, this word, if unaccompanied by any qualifying epithet, should be used only to signify positive law as above described. This is the sense in which the word is employed by writers on Jurisprudence and for the most part also by practising lawyers. In this sense, moreover, law is distinguished satisfactorily from the other influences which have to be considered. On the other hand, if the word is used with any wider meaning ambiguity almost inevitably results.[2]

---

[1] *Jurisprudence*, 5th ed. vol. i. p. 220.

[2] It is generally assumed by jurists that law can exist only in a state ; and that to the existence of a state a considerable population as well as a certain degree of organization on a territorial basis are necessary. Accordingly, rules promulgated by the chieftain of a nomadic tribe, or of any community too small in point of numbers to be regarded as a state, would not be ' laws ' in the received meaning of the word, although they were enforced by the supreme power of the particular society. Such rules may therefore be considered as falling into a separate category of their own. But, for the purposes of this treatise, there is no essential or practical importance in this distinction ; and it is sufficient to forestall what would at the best be a merely verbal criticism.

The Social Imperative

Social intercourse necessarily results in the erection of standards for its own regulation. Every society develops a common perception of what is correct conduct in the relations of the members to one another. Conduct of the kind which is approved by the general sentiment is in a sense prescribed by the common will of the community. The principles thus evolved are recognized as obligatory by its individual members whenever they consciously advert to them. They feel that it would be unworthy of themselves to disregard the standard of behaviour in the society to which they belong ; and they know that any overt contravention of that standard would draw down upon them the disapprobation of their fellows. For the most part, however, the prevailing principles of conduct are followed by well-disposed and normal people as a matter of course without the exercise of any conscious election. Conduct of the kind prescribed is, indeed, largely a matter of habit or even of nature.

The principles thus evolved concern matters of the gravest moment as well as those of comparatively trivial character. Morality (in the popular sense of the word), humanity, honour, etiquette, fashion, and ' good form ' are comprised within them. Moreover, for the most part, positive laws and customary rules are reinforced by the sanction of this social standard ; while, to a great extent, its dictates correspond with those of the individual conscience. In the opinion of the present writer this system may conveniently be called ' The Social Imperative.' [1]

In one of the comparatively few dissertations in which this subject has been specifically dealt with by Englishmen the scope and nature of this imperative are explained as follows : The field of daily conduct ' is covered, in the case of the citizen, only to a small extent by law and legality on the one hand, and by the dictates of the individual conscience on the other. There is a more extensive system of guidance which regulates conduct and which differs from both in its character and sanction. It applies, like law, to all the members of a society alike, without distinction of persons. It resembles the morality of conscience in that it is enforced by no legal compulsion. . . . The system is so generally accepted, and is held in so high regard, that no one can venture to disregard it without in some way suffering at the hands of his neighbours for so doing. If a man maltreats his wife and children, or habitually jostles his fellow-citizen in the street, or does things flagrantly selfish or in bad taste, he is pretty sure to find himself in a minority and the worse off in the end. Not only does it not pay to do these things, but the decent man does not wish to do them. . . . The guide to which the citizen mostly looks is just the standard recognized by the community, a community made up mainly of those fellow-citizens

[1] Lord Haldane, writing to the author on reading the first edition of this work, said : ' The " Social Imperative " is a new phrase in this connexion, and I think a very good one.'

whose good opinion he respects and desires to have.' [1]

The Social Imperative is, accordingly, the main influence whereby the conduct of the citizen is regulated. In all ordinary circumstances a normal Englishman acts, as a matter of habit and without specially adverting to the foundations of his duty, in accordance with the sentiments and views of his fellow-countrymen. He speaks the truth without effort ; he fulfils his engagements as a matter of course ; he dresses himself in apparel similar to that worn by other members of his class with the same regularity of routine as that with which he takes his ordinary meals ; if a passing stranger slips by the way, he helps him up as the result of a volition as instinctive as that which would extend his arm in order to break his own fall. Negatively, he is no more inclined to kill or maim his neighbour than he is to injure himself. This disposition—this habitual mental and moral attitude—in so far as it is caused by anything external to his own conscience, is in the main the result of the prevailing sentiment of the society to which he belongs. The community wills or commands that the conduct of its members should be in harmony with its social feelings ; and, by the collective will of

[1] Lord Haldane's Address to the American Bar Association at Montreal on 1st September 1913. In that address it was pointed out that Fichte describes this system as ' those principles of conduct which regulate people in their relations to each other, and which have become matter of habit and second nature at the stage of culture reached, and of which, therefore, we are not explicitly conscious.' Cf. Holland's *Jurisprudence*, 13th ed. pp. 27–31.

the community, its members are individually constrained.

Public Opinion

When any one shapes his conduct according to the views or judgment on a particular matter of those among whom he lives, he defers to the authority of Public Opinion.

In so far as a probable consequence of conduct opposed to Public Opinion is the disapproval of an indeterminate number of the members of the community in question, there is an analogy between the sanction of this authority and that of Custom and the Social Imperative. The important distinctions by which it is separated from them are these. Custom and the Social Imperative are for the most part gradually developed ; they are generally followed subconsciously ; and they prescribe general rules. On the other hand, Public Opinion is a more or less deliberate exercise of judgment or will, or conscious inclination of feeling ; the deference to its authority is to a large extent the result of advertence to its existence ; and its subject-matter is a particular state of facts. The facts may be of the most complicated character : they may comprise, for example, the administration of a group of statutes or the policy of the State towards another Power. But Public Opinion is essentially *ad hoc*. It consists rather of particular commands than of a body of general rules of conduct. Moreover, while Custom and the Social Imperative, to a very large extent, embody the result of the habits and the views of past generations which have been adopted without any consideration of their merits by the living, Public Opinion consists primarily of the views or sentiments of the living themselves.

The existence and efficacy of Public Opinion depend largely upon the extent and rapidity of the communication which takes place between the various members of a society. It is comprehensive and potent in small communities and also in the later stages of modern civilization ; while it is comparatively limited in scope and weak in operation during the intermediate phases of national development.

Thus in the case, for example, of a Saxon tribe before the Anglo-Saxon settlement in England, Public Opinion was probably so general and constant in its operation as practically to coalesce with, or at all events largely to overlap, some of the other regulating influences which we have reviewed. The assembly of the freemen—combining the leading characteristics of both a legislature and a public meeting—would naturally lead to a highly developed Public Opinion. But in the days of the Conqueror or of the earlier Plantagenets it is obvious that, owing to the want of efficient means of communication between the residents in different parts of the country as well as to the relatively depressed condition of the majority of the inhabitants, Public Opinion, as an influence upon conduct, outside comparatively narrow limits, must have been at a very low ebb.

' While holding,' says Herbert Spencer,[1] ' that, in unorganized groups of men, the feeling manifested as public opinion controls political conduct,

[1] *Principles of Sociology*, vol. ii. p. 325.

just as it controls the conduct distinguished as ceremonial and religious ; and while holding that governing agencies, during their early stages, are at once the products of aggregate feeling, derive their powers from it, and are restrained by it ; we must admit that these primitive relations become complicated when, by war, small groups are compounded and re-compounded into great ones. When the society is largely composed of subjugated people held down by superior force, the normal relation . . . no longer exists. We must not expect to find in a rule coercively established by an invader the same traits as in a rule that has grown up from within. Societies formed by conquest may be, and frequently are, composed of two societies, which are in large measure, if not entirely, alien ; and in them there cannot arise a political force from the aggregate will. Under such conditions the political head either derives his power exclusively from the feeling of the dominant class, or else, setting the diverse feelings originated in the upper and lower classes one against the other, is enabled so to make his individual will the chief factor.'

For the last century or so Public Opinion has occupied a large place in the life of the English people, and its influence is still increasing in our own time. The working of representative institutions, which have now reached an advanced stage of development in connexion with the central legislature, as well as local administrative bodies all over the land ; the general ability of the people as the result of education to understand public affairs and form intelligent views with regard to them ; the practice of holding public meetings and of discussing political topics wherever men meet together in social intercourse ; wireless broadcasting ; and, above all, perhaps, the almost universal habit of reading newspapers, which in themselves are, in one aspect, competitive reflectors of the views of their readers, appear to be bringing the influence of Public Opinion to a condition of pre-eminent potency in the control alike of governments, classes, and individuals.

PROPOSITION VIII.—The conduct of individual men is controlled externally by unregulated force, administrative authority, sacerdotal authority, custom, convention, positive law, the social imperative, and public opinion.

CHAPTER IX

THE CONTROL OF STATES

F
ROM the fact that states are corporations of which the members are human beings, it naturally follows that they are, for the most part, subject to the operation of forces and influences corresponding to those by which the conduct of individuals is regulated.[1] It is essential for our present purpose to understand the precise extent of this correspondence and also to form an adequate conception of the consequences of its failure in one important particular.

EXTRANEOUS FORCE

States are influenced in their conduct by the existence of the force of other states, just as individual men are influenced by the force residing in others of their own kind.

A small community does not lightly attack, or bear itself in a menacing attitude, towards a Great Power. Any state, indeed, before embarking upon hostilities against another, takes into consideration

[1] It may, however, be convenient to bear in mind that a state differs from a natural person in the following important respects : (1) Being an artificial entity it is susceptible of division ; (2) It has no existence apart from the possession of territory ; and (3) Its welfare is not an end in itself : it exists only for the purpose of promoting the happiness of its citizens.

the force which it appears to possess.[1] No state acts as if other states had no force which they could exercise upon occasion.

In innumerable instances, indeed, particular states must have been deterred from aggressions which in themselves seemed desirable by an appreciation of the risk of encountering the power of those states which might otherwise have been their prey.

The restraining influence of this force, although necessarily indefinite and of varying strength, is continuously operative. Moreover, when it is associated with circumstances which constitute a balance of power as between the leading states, history shows that it may be an important factor in the preservation of an equilibrium for a considerable period.

ADMINISTRATIVE AUTHORITY

The control which has often been exercised in many ways by large states over smaller communities presents a close analogy to the administrative or arbitrary control exercised in the form of occasional or particular commands by an individual superior over his inferior, or by a governing body over those who are subject to its authority.

The perception of this control is largely obscured by the theoretical limitation of the cognizance of International Law to sovereign states or communities of analogous character, and by the juristic theory of the equality and independence of all such states. It should, however, be obvious that, in substance and in fact, this kind of authority has

[1] Cf. Luke xiv. 31, 32.

6

often been exercised by one state over another, sometimes in pursuance of suzerainty or a protectorate ; sometimes in pursuance of a hegemony assumed by the former over the race to which the latter belongs ; and sometimes without any special claim or pretext of right.

Moreover, in modern times, control of this character has been extensively exercised by the Great Powers collectively over the smaller states. In illustration of this, it may be sufficient here to cite the following passages with reference to the action of the Concert of Europe from the time of the battle of Waterloo from Dr. T. J. Lawrence's work on *The Principles of International Law*.[1]

' At the beginning of the last century a certain leadership was assumed by a group of powers who had borne the brunt of the struggle against Napoleon. At the Congress of Vienna in 1814 and 1815, France, conquered though she was, succeeded in gaining a place by their side, and in 1818 she was formally admitted to an equal share in their deliberations and decisions. Thus was constituted the Concert of Europe. It consisted originally of England, France, Austria, Prussia (since merged in Germany), and Russia, and in 1867 the newly created kingdom of Italy was added. It has passed through periods of greater and lesser vigour ; but, if now and again it has seemed for a time to be in abeyance, it has always reasserted its position and authority. To describe its activity with fullness would be to write a large part of the international history of Europe during a century crowded with great events. . . . The Great Powers

[1] 7th ed. pp. 246–7.

. . . called into being the European order that succeeded the wars of the French Revolution and the conquests of Napoleon, and have supervised many of the important modifications of it which have since taken place. The kingdom of Greece has grown up under the tutelage of the European Concert, which has more than once restrained it, once secured for it additional territory, and once at least preserved it from destruction. . . . In the case of Belgium, all the Great Powers were formally concerned from the first in its severance from Holland, and all concurred in its neutralization as an independent state in 1839. One of the main objects of the Crimean War, and the only one that has been permanently attained, was to take the power of settling the destinies of the subject Christian populations of Turkey out of the hands of Russia alone, and entrust it instead to the Concert of Europe. Though Austria and Prussia had not been belligerents, they were admitted as Great Powers to the conference that drew up the Treaty of Paris in 1856. And again, in 1878, Russia was not allowed to impose her own terms on Turkey, but they were submitted to a conference, in which England, France, Germany, Austria, and Italy took part, though none of them had been engaged in the conflict. The Congress discussed exhaustively the questions raised by the war, and substituted the Treaty of Berlin for the Treaty of San Stefano, which was regarded as a preliminary document to be modified by general consent. The readjustments that have taken place since have been matters of negotiation between the powers ; and the last and greatest of them, the annexation of Bosnia and Herzegovina by Austria in 1908, gave rise to an acute controversy. . . . In addition to superintending and controlling the territorial and political changes we have described, the Great Powers received Turkey into the family of nations in 1856, made provision in the same year for the due execution of international works at the mouth of the Danube, conferred the rank of a Great Power on Italy and neutralized Luxemburg in 1867, and granted conditional recognition of independence to Roumania, Serbia, and Montenegro in 1878.'

The deficiencies of the Concert of the Powers as an administrative body are manifest. This Concert has never rested, like the government of a well-ordered state, upon the foundation of a full and unquestioned supremacy supported by laws systematically enforced. It has not operated readily and efficiently on all occasions when peace has been threatened. In particular, it has not been by any means uniformly successful in avoiding hostilities between its own members.

In the present position of international affairs, however, we ought not to lose sight of its great value in the past and of the possibilities of its development in the future, which will be considered more fully hereafter. It is of great importance to recognize that, as we shall see in the chapter on International Law, this system fails to cover many of the most important aspects of the relations of states, and accordingly that there is wide scope for the exercise of some administrative authority in the great society which they collectively compose. The constitution of an appropriate organ of such authority is indeed the one crucial difficulty which mankind have still to overcome in their quest of permanent peace.

SACERDOTAL AUTHORITY

In the Middle Ages this kind of authority was frequently exercised over states and their rulers. And, even in our own time, if the world as a whole were surveyed, it would not be difficult to find instances of deference to such authority.

CUSTOM

The history of the relations of states and the body of usages which form the substratum of what is called ' International Law ' show very clearly the importance of custom in the regulation of the conduct of states.   Owing to the universal disposition of mankind to establish customary rules, it could not be otherwise.   International usages will be considered hereafter in Chapter XII.

CONVENTION

Treaties have played a part in the regulation of the relations of states closely analogous to that of contract in the sphere of civil life.

' Fundamentum autem justitiæ est fides, id est dictorum conventorumque constantia et veritas.'   The truth conveyed in this statement of Cicero [1] has been generally recognized by the conscience of mankind as equally applicable to justice between state and state and man and man.   ' Upon a scrupulous

[1] *De Officiis*, lib. i. 7.

fidelity in the observation of treaties, not merely in their letter but in their spirit, obviously depends, under God, the peace of the world. *Pacta sunt servanda* is the pervading maxim of International, as it was of Roman jurisprudence. The treaty-breaking state is the great enemy of nations, the disturber of their peace, the destroyer of their happiness, the obstacle to their progress.' [1]

' If faith be taken away, as Aristotle says, the intercourse of men is abolished. . . . And this the supreme rulers of mankind ought to be more careful of preserving, in proportion as they have more impunity for their violations of it ; so that if faith be taken away they will be like wild beasts, whose strength is an object of general horror. And in other parts of its sphere justice has often some-what that is obscure, but the bond of good faith is manifest of itself and indeed is used to remove obscurity from all other matters.' [2]

THE SOCIAL IMPERATIVE

The operation of this kind of authority over states is rapidly increasing both in extent and in efficiency.

The governments of states generally speaking refrain from conduct towards other states which would be universally regarded as improper or dis-honourable. They also habitually do many things in the interest of other states which are required of them by the general sentiment of civilized mankind.

[1] Phillimore's *International Law*, 3rd ed. vol. ii. pp. 69, 70.
[2] Grotius, *De Jure Belli et Pacis*, bk. iii. ch. xxv. 1, 2 (Whewell's translation).

The scope and efficacy of this imperative must depend upon the extent to which a common sense or will is developed on the part of the peoples of the different states ; and this development will closely follow the approximation of their respective modes of thought and moral standards.   This approximation in turn will largely depend upon the extent of their intercommunication and their consequent action and reaction upon one another.

In other words, a common will or sentiment on the part of the states of the world will be developed to an extent corresponding from time to time to that to which they become associated as a true community or society.

The development of this Social Imperative will indeed for the most part proceed *pari passu* with that of an international Public Opinion.

PUBLIC OPINION

The rapidity with which information can now be circulated throughout the civilized world and views and comments thereon exchanged between the inhabitants of different hemispheres ; the general practice among the more advanced peoples of reading newspapers ; the increasing importance and variety of interests common to the various races ; the facilities for travel ; wireless broad-casting and the character of modern life in general, tend to produce conditions in which the formation of a true international opinion becomes possible throughout a constantly widening area.   The discoveries of science, and other achievements in the direction of material progress, have to a very large extent cleared the way for a momentous moral advance on the part of mankind collectively.

Everything indeed which tends to facilitate the diffusion of accurate information upon contemporary events, or which assists the several communities of mankind to apprehend it correctly, and therefore similarly, must increase the probability of the formation of a common understanding as to the moral aspects of current discussions.   In this connexion it would seem that still greater frankness and less secrecy in the diplomatic intercourse between governments than is yet universal would assist in promoting a sound international opinion with regard to the relations between states.   In this respect, as in most others, the advantages of publicity are now so obvious and so great that very special and cogent reasons must be forthcoming in order that they may really be countervailed.

In short, the greater the extent to which the minds of mankind at large are applied to the consideration of the same facts at the same time, the more comprehensive and effective will be the body of opinion which they will from time to time collectively form.

In one aspect, the state of contemporary opinion throughout the world since the outbreak of the Great War has marked a considerable advance in the direction of a common feeling and judgment on the part of mankind at large.   Never before did so many human beings take an interest in one and the same series of contemporary events.   Never before were so many millions in divers lands substantially of one mind with regard to their interest and duty in matters of common concern.

On the whole it would seem that we are warranted in basing great hopes upon the development of both Public Opinion and the Social Imperative throughout the society of states.   The operation of these influences on the several communities should not be substantially different either in its character or effect from that of the analogous influences in a particular state upon its own citizens.   There can indeed be no well-founded doubt that a comprehensive, alert, and articulate international opinion, and a strong and healthy social sense pervading the civilized world, will be potent influences in the direction of the preservation of peace.

So far we have seen that the conduct of states is controlled by authorities and influences which are essentially similar to those by which the conduct of individuals is regulated.   We must now note the important respect in which this correspondence is not found.

POSITIVE LAW

Positive Law is, as we have seen, dependent upon the existence of the controlling power in a state.   Those to whom it applies must be subject to a common authority charged with the enforcement of its provisions.   Owing to the absence of a common sovereignty over the society of states, the necessary condition to the existence therein of positive law is wanting.   Accordingly, Law, in the strict and definite meaning of the term, is not among the resources available for the preservation of peace.   But, as will appear in Chapter XI, the gap thus left in the system whereby the conduct of states is regulated does not constitute an insurmountable difficulty in the way of preventing wars.

The question thus arises : By what means can the functions of law and governmental administration within a state be best fulfilled in the great society of states themselves ? In other words, in what way can we best develop an adequate sanction for Public Right and at the same time provide for the proper and effective administration of common affairs of vital importance to the welfare and order of the society of states ?

PROPOSITION IX.—All the means whereby the conduct of individuals is regulated, except positive law, are available for the preservation of peace in the society of states.

CHAPTER X

THE RELATION OF LAW TO ORDER

WE have seen that it is not at present practicable to bring the society of states into full subjection to a common sovereignty, and accordingly that, if peace is to be established in our own time, it must be by virtue of means other than those of positive law.

It therefore becomes important to form a just conception of the value of law in relation to society, as compared with the other forces and influences whereby human conduct is regulated. In this connexion it will be useful to consider whether the future progress of men, even when regarded as the citizens of particular communities, will depend mainly upon the development and perfecting of the reign of law as we now understand it ; or whether the function of law is in a sense transitory—whether, indeed, when men have attained to the full height of their moral nature, the reign of law will be universal or whether it will have been entirely or to any considerable extent superseded by other influences. It is conceived that the examination of these questions will materially further the inquiry as to the practicability and the means of establishing peace on earth.

There can be no doubt that law has for some thousands of years been a factor of paramount importance in the development of civilization Adapting a Pauline metaphor for our purpose we may say that it has been a schoolmaster by whose discipline men have been trained to just and orderly behaviour.

In our own country this has been the case to a pre-eminent degree. Englishmen indeed have generally felt that the greatness of their nation was largely due to the prevalent respect for law. At a relatively early stage of their history they learned to regard it as the beneficent alternative to despotism as well as to anarchy. By virtue of its general sway they perceived that the worst features of arbitrary government were excluded from their civic life ; while violent self-redress of injuries was rendered unnecessary through the provision of adequate and assured remedies in courts of justice. The obligation of agreements between man and man was at the same time firmly upheld. Accordingly for many centuries the fact that a rule was understood to be ' the law ' generally ensured for it the respect of the people at large. Even where neither the provisions of the rule in question nor the manner of its presentment were in themselves calculated to secure admiration or approval reasonable men usually felt constrained to implicit obedience. The law was moreover a terror to evil-doers. While they sought to elude the vigilance of its ministers, the system itself they regarded with genuine awe.

This being so, laymen, speaking generally, never doubted that the prevalence of law was an essential condition of social life and prosperity. In their eyes national improvement appeared to depend upon the amelioration of the law and the increasing disposition of the community to obey its dictates for the time being. With this view jurists naturally felt complete professional sympathy. To layman and lawyer alike the absolute reign of a beneficent legal system appeared to be in the nature of an ultimate ideal.

We must, however, carefully consider whether the present attitude of society and its apparent tendencies support this view, or whether they do not rather suggest that it will gradually be essentially transformed.

To what extent then is the conduct of the ordinary good citizen at the present day affected by law ? In other words, bearing in mind that ' the most obvious characteristic of law is that it is coercive,' [1] to what extent does it cause such a citizen to behave differently from the way in which he would behave if all the rules comprised in the system were merely the recognized enunciation of prevalent opinion, or even were not in existence at all as definitely formulated propositions ?

Such a citizen recognizes without question the obligation *in foro conscientiæ* of fulfilling his business engagements. ' *Pactum serva*,' the motto of the great Plantagenet, is among the earliest lessons assimilated by infant intelligence in this country, and is so well established as a governing principle of conduct by the time maturity is reached that its operation is as easy and almost as unnoticed as that of a primordial instinct. The average householder pays his agreed rent and discharges his tradesmen's bills without adverting to the

[1] Holland's *Jurisprudence*, 13th ed. p. 79.

legal necessity for doing so. To him they are essentially, and in the natural sense of the words, debts of honour, and he would not be comfortable if they were not punctually paid. Only when some question arises as to the scope of his agreed liability is any difficulty likely to occur between himself and his creditor. If the parties are then reasonable, as well as honest, their difference may be amicably settled by themselves. Otherwise it has to be adjusted by some one else. So far, indeed, as contractual relations are concerned, the function of law in its actual operation is for the most part limited, as regards good citizens, to the provision of a system of judicature, whereby the decision of a competent and trusted third party may be obtained in cases where the interpretation of a bargain, or its application to certain facts which have ensued, is open to honest doubt.

When we turn to the law of torts and the law of crimes, the subordinate part played by the coercive character of law is still more evident. No respectable man has any inclination to kill, or imprison, or wound, or, under ordinary circumstances, to assault his neighbour ; or to steal or injure his property ; or to impair his reputation ; or maliciously and without reasonable cause to prosecute him ; or to destroy his domestic happiness. Nor does the just man need to be constrained by legal sanctions to be careful not to run his fellow-citizen down on the highway ; or, if any one is entrusted to his care or skill, whether as the driver of a conveyance, or as a surgeon or otherwise, to discharge the trust reposed in him by a due display of the care and skill demanded by the occasion.

Accordingly, at the present time, the will or conduct of the average citizen is not ordinarily, in any active sense, compelled or governed by the law of torts or the law of crimes.

In regard to certain matters, indeed, it is necessary that there should be a prescribed course of conduct, because the general welfare is dependent upon uniformity of action therein on the part of all. Thus in any country where there are well-defined roads it is essential that there should be a rule for the guidance of those who use them. The importance of the rule as such, apart from its intrinsic merits, is obvious from the fact that the necessary uniformity of conduct is secured in one country by prescribing the right side of the road and in another the left. In all such cases, however, the good citizen complies with the rule without any sense of being constrained to do so by the fear of the penalty attached to disobedience. He does as a matter of course that which is obviously right under the circumstances in which he finds himself.

Accordingly, it appears that conscience and the social imperative are usually sufficient in themselves to keep the good citizen in the paths prescribed by law.

And as his own behaviour becomes progressively less dependent upon the sanctions of the legal system, so his reliance upon these sanctions for the enforcement of the good behaviour of others towards himself diminishes also.

So far as the realm of contracts is concerned, correlatively to what has been said above, it would appear that the law is practically invoked by such citizens only where an engagement is of doubtful interpretation or effect or where it has been entered into with a dishonest person.

With regard to torts and crimes it is no doubt clear that ordinary citizens in the present state of society would incur grave risks if the sanctions of law were altogether absent. Owing to the number of people who are still of evil disposition, or who do not habitually obey an enlightened conscience, and the fact that the means of self-redress or defence have, as it were, long been suffered to fall into abeyance, the coercive character of law is still important in this connexion.

But, even here, we may discern a weakening in the reliance upon law. Many a householder, on being disturbed by the sounds of the operations of burglars, thinks rather of his policy of assurance than of the capture of the offenders. And the state itself is now becoming sparing in its use of terrors as deterrents from crime. Punishment is ceasing to be vindictive ; and there is a tendency to regard crime as a symptom of a pathological condition, and the criminal as a subject for curative treatment.

The apparent decline in the relative importance of law is, moreover, very marked in connexion with the department of the system which concerns the relations between the Crown and the Executive Government on the one hand and the subject on the other. The security which the latter enjoys against arbitrary treatment at the hands of the former now lies rather in public opinion than in any of the provisions of Magna Charta or sub-sequent statutory enactments or judicial precedents. Various Acts and Orders passed during the War, and the administration of the powers thereby conferred upon civil and military functionaries, constituted a very striking and conclusive demonstration of this fact.

There appear, then, to be indications that the common weal of Englishmen is now dependent upon law to a less extent than was formerly the case. The same is probably equally true, *mutatis mutandis*, of the citizens of all advanced states.[1]

It also appears quite clear that the respect for law is now less than it formerly was. Not only has its sanction become weaker but its prestige has diminished.

From time to time numbers of honest people in this country have persistently disobeyed particular laws of which they disapproved. But in recent times many have gone much further than this and have committed breaches of existing laws of which they did not disapprove because they desired a particular new law to be passed by Parliament. Nothing of this kind, or at all events no such conduct on the same extensive scale, took place in earlier stages of our national life. But, judging from the way in which attempts to promote what those who made them believed to be good objects in illegal ways were dealt with formerly, it may reasonably be supposed that any similar conduct would then have been met by the imposition on the part of the legislature or the judiciary of penalties of exceptional severity. The attempt to attain a general public

[1] The extent to which civilized man is emancipated from the need for positive law was well illustrated by the conditions of life in Spitzbergen for many years before its acquisition by Norway.

7

object by forcible methods, as late as, say, the beginning of the eighteenth century, and perhaps long after, would probably have been pronounced constructive treason and punished accordingly. Nowadays a quite opposite course is taken. The ordinary penalties attached by the law to transgressions of the class in question are either entirely waived or mitigated to a point at which they cease to be deterrent. Such occurrences suggest that England, to speak only of this country for the moment, is approaching a condition of general feeling in which it may be impracticable to enforce any law against the organized resistance of a section of the population which is at the same time considerable in numbers and respectable in point of general reputation.

The decline of law in the estimation of the people admits of explanation.

The respect with which law was formerly regarded was due largely to a certain mystery which obscured its origin. Its substratum was supposed to be the immemorial usages of the race—the customs of remote ancestors. Its exponents were imposing personages, surrounded by much pomp and ceremony, whose proceedings in the administration of their criminal jurisdiction were characterized by relentless severity. Even in so far as the law had been embodied in statutes of the realm, it was the work for the most part of sages and magnates whose social rank elevated them far above the average plain citizen. It is true that occasionally the provisions of a statute gave effect to a really popular demand. But, until the time of the Reform Act of 1832, the legislation of Parliament was for the most part more or less the work of lawyers and other experts with the assistance of members of the aristocratic classes. To the multitude the law as a whole was characterized by the awfulness of a majesty concealed in the darkness of the unknown and the unknowable.

The extension of the franchise, working in conjunction with the absolutely unlimited supremacy of Parliament in the United Kingdom, produced in these respects a fundamental change. Since 1832 the great activity of the legislature and its reflection of public opinion have gradually brought home to the mind of the ordinary citizen the fact that the law is largely the embodiment of the opinions of people like himself, and that it lies within the power of a majority of the electors to make it whatever they please.

' In England . . . the beliefs or sentiments which, during the nineteenth century, have governed the development of the law have in strictness been public opinion, for they have been the wishes and ideas as to legislation held by the people of England, or, to speak with more precision, by the majority of those citizens who have at a given moment taken an effective part in public life.' [1]   ' The close and immediate connexion . . . which in modern England exists between public opinion and legislation is a very peculiar and noteworthy fact, to which we cannot easily find a parallel. Nowhere have changes in popular convictions or wishes found anything like such rapid and immediate expression in alterations of the law as they have in Great Britain during the nineteenth

[1] Dicey's *Law and Opinion in England*, pp. 9–10.

century, and more especially during the last half thereof.' [1]

It might have been thought that law, when recognized as the will of the majority of the community, would have appeared more truly worthy of respect than it did in its earlier aspect of clouded mystery. But a little consideration will show that the contrary must be the case. Indeed, paradoxical as it may sound, the truth is that the more thoroughly law is recognized to be in conformity with public opinion the less will be its authority as law.

The general coincidence of law with public opinion indirectly causes the growth of a sentiment that any inconsistency is mischievous. The rapidity with which public opinion is usually reflected in the law develops an impatience when such reflection is delayed. The personal share of the elector in the process of legislation precludes any superstitious veneration on his own part for the result. The more plainly it is seen that law rests upon the consent of the people, the greater is the tendency for those who disapprove of any of its provisions to lose their respect for its authority.

But more than this. The greater the extent to which, and the rapidity with which, public opinion is embodied in law, the greater is the tendency for public opinion—apart from its enactment by the legislature—to become the real authority, to which men readily defer. As soon as they feel that it is certain that public opinion will speedily become law, a natural tendency is set up to regard public opinion itself as the really important and substantial matter and law as mainly formal. Thus public

[1] Dicey's *Law and Opinion in England*, p. 7.

opinion is obeyed before it becomes law, while there is a tendency to cease to obey the law in so far as it fails to embody public opinion. In other words, he who regards law as in its essence formulated public opinion may easily be led to repudiate the obligatory effect of a statute the provisions of which he thinks are at variance with that opinion.

But even where the law is coincident with general opinion it is not beyond the reach of processes whereby its authority is being undermined.

' With progress,' says Herbert Spencer, ' towards a popular form of government . . . though the obligation to do this and refrain from that is held to arise from state-enactment ; yet the authority which gives this enactment its force is the public desire. Still it is observable that along with a tacit implication that the *consensus* of individual interests affords the warrant for law, there goes the overt assertion that this warrant is derived from the formulated will of the majority ; no question being raised whether this formulated will is or is not congruous with the *consensus* of individual interests. In this current theory there obviously survives the old idea that there is no other sanction for law than the command of embodied authority ; though the authority is now a widely different one. But this theory . . . is a transitional theory. The ultimate theory, which it foreshadows, is that the source of legal obligation is the *consensus* of individual interests itself, and not the will of a majority determined by their opinion concerning it ; which may or may not be right. . . . Already in respect of religious opinions there is practically conceded the right of the individual to disobey the law, even though it expresses the will of a majority. . . . These ideas and feelings are all significant of progress towards the view, proper to the developed industrial state, that the justification for a law is that it enforces one or other of the conditions to harmonious social co-operation ; and that it is unjustified (enacted by no matter how high an authority or how general an opinion) if it traverses these conditions. And this is tantamount to saying that the impersonally derived law which revives as personally derived law declines, and which gives expression to the *consensus* of individual interests, becomes, in its final form, simply an applied system of ethics —or rather of that part of ethics which concerns men's just relations with one another and with the community.' [1]

The fact, however, that the decline of the respect for law admits of these explanations by no means deprives this decline of its significance. There is no room for reasonable doubt that the present inhabitants of this country are in a state of moral development higher than that of their ancestors at any period since the various races to which they owe their origin were fused into one. Accordingly, if their future progress were mainly dependent upon law it might reasonably have been expected that their respect for law would have been greater than that of their predecessors. The evidence that the contrary is the case, and that, indeed, the respect for law is still declining, appears to suggest that the promise of the future lies mainly with other agencies than that of law.

The progressive emancipation of civilized man

[1] *Principles of Sociology*, vol. ii. pp. 533-4.

from the necessity for law is moreover not confined to its coercive aspect as a system resting upon external sanctions.

The more highly developed a human being is, the less is the need for providing him with an elaborate code of rules. The tendency of moral progress is to cause the merger of multitudinous regulations—for practical purposes—into a few guiding and comprehensive principles which assist the conscience of the individual and tend to become incorporated in the social imperative. Of many possible illustrations of this process it may suffice here to indicate two.

In the Old Testament and the Rabbinical writings a body of rules and regulations was provided for the guidance of the conduct of the Jews which was so large that none but persons specially skilled therein would have been likely to have a thorough mastery of the whole. But the duty of man to his fellow-creatures was summarized by Christ in a very few words : ' As ye would that men should do to you, do ye also to them likewise.' [1]

In England the laws of contracts, torts, and crimes are not fully ascertainable without reference to books which are so numerous and widely scattered that no living lawyer could possibly be familiar with them all. But, for the practical purposes of the honest man, may not their purport be conveyed adequately thus : ' Keep your promise and injure no one ' ?

It seems, therefore, that, as mankind progress, they become less dependent for their welfare and peace upon the specific provisions of elaborate

[1] Luke vi. 31.

systems of jurisprudence. More and more they are able to rely, for the guidance of their ordinary conduct as individuals, upon the broad principles illuminating the active conscience and the unceasing direction of the social imperative. During the countless generations for which men have lived together in communities they have in fact been gradually learning the obligations which result from social existence, and their perception of these has become a part of their developed nature.[1]

It may then be concluded that the prime virtue of positive law lies in its operation as an indispensable specific against wrongdoing in a certain stage of social evolution.

After any particular community has ceased to consist only of a small horde whose feelings could be manifested at a meeting attended by all, a period must usually follow when public opinion is more or less in abeyance and the social imperative is inadequate to the regulation of daily life and conduct. And until the community acquires an advanced civilization, with the accompanying facilities for communication and the diffusion of information and a degree of education and intelligence commensurate with the enlarged scope and varied character of its common affairs, it cannot regain a public opinion or develop a social imperative

[1] On the other hand, it is important to bear in mind, in connexion with the subject of this treatise, that the requirements of any community collectively are continually changing. Accordingly, the necessity for ordinances of an administrative character, prescribing from time to time the obligations of the citizen to the community—his contributions to central and local expenditure, his personal services to the state, and the like—continues in full operation.

adequate for the prevention of wrongdoing. If during this period order is to be established and maintained, positive law enforced by a central government must prevail. So long as other means of regulating conduct are insufficient, the existence of law is necessary for the purpose of providing a standing probability that evil consequences will be suffered by transgressors.

It is quite clear that, down to our own time, law has been essential to national life and progress in England. And many years must elapse before it will cease to be necessary either in this country or elsewhere. Possibly, indeed, long ages will pass away before the whole of mankind will have outgrown its uses. Nevertheless, viewing the world at large, it may safely be said that the importance of law is steadily diminishing. The apprehension of the sentence of a Court of Justice as a motive to right conduct is being replaced by deference to a rule or mandate which is felt to be in itself obligatory, either as the ordinance of the will of society or as the direction of the individual conscience. The extent of the dominion of the social imperative, public opinion, and conscience is steadily increasing.

In this connexion it is to be observed that, while it may be anticipated that the development of the society of states will, to some extent, be analogous to that of a society of individual men, no exact correspondence is probable or indeed possible. Two reasons for divergencies are apparent. In the first place, as we have seen, the development of a community of individuals into the highly organized form of society called a state has been almost everywhere due to the exigencies of defence against other societies ; whereas, from the nature of the case, outside the community of states as a whole no other society could exist.   In the second place, the development of particular states as such has been for the most part by no means dependent upon the previous existence among their peoples, as a condition precedent thereto, of any advanced civilization or the prevalence of an elevated standard of morality. On the other hand, the development of a true social order throughout the society of states will be possible only when mankind shall have attained a stage of moral advancement higher than any which has hitherto been reached.

Accordingly, it is not to be inferred from the necessary function of law in the development of particular states that it will have a similar function with regard to the development of a world-wide society.

PROPOSITION X.—The importance of positive law in the regulation of the conduct of civilized mankind tends to diminish.

CHAPTER XI

THE ESSENTIAL SANCTION

IN the present stage of the moral progress of mankind it is still true of any large community that the direction of the individual conscience and the impulse of the social sense are in themselves insufficient to secure the general welfare and maintain permanent order. Some external restraining force—some sanction of general rules of conduct and administrative orders—remains an essential element in social life as at present constituted.

We have seen that, for the most part, the actions of men are carried out without conscious advertence to any obligatory motive for performing them. But every one occasionally engages in reflection before he determines upon a particular line of conduct. In such instances an ordinary citizen will generally form his decision in accordance with the social sense of the community to which he belongs so far as it is immanent in himself. He will do what he believes is becoming in him as a citizen, or as a gentleman, a professional man, a public official, a trader, a workman, or a servant, as the case may be. He will act with what he deems to be propriety, or good taste, or good form, or in accordance with honour or the social duty of one who occupies his particular situation in the world.

In some cases, however, he will advert to the still higher authority of his own individual conscience and will do what he conceives to be right according to that supreme standard. But, in exceptional cases, such a citizen, owing to the effect of anger or some other specially disturbing cause, may be so strongly inclined to act in contravention of his social sense and even of his conscience that the mere risk of his own self-disapprobation would not be sufficient to deter him from such action. If, under these circumstances, he is to keep in the right path, his will must yield to a direction which is imperative by virtue of the fact that it is supported by a sanction external to himself.

What then is the essential characteristic of this regulating factor which society everywhere provides as a prime necessity of its own orderly existence ?

In the case supposed, the citizen apprehends that, if he contravenes the social will of the community, he will probably incur evil consequences at the hands of that community, the collective power of which is greater than his own. Such consequences will vary in certain important particulars according to the kind of conduct which is in question. If positive law concurs with the social imperative in forbidding it, they will consist primarily of a penalty, the extent of which is not generally precisely determined in advance, pronounced by a Court of Justice and carried into effect by executive officials of a certain class. If it is otherwise, the probable consequences will consist mainly of an indefinite penalty, such as, for example, being ' cut,' censured, boycotted, hustled, or even subjected to the last extremity of personal violence, inflicted by persons who cannot be determined with precision beforehand. A breach of the law as such involves the legal sanction ; a breach of the social imperative as such involves the social sanction. The law and the social will respectively are imperative by virtue of these sanctions. In most cases the law, and in many cases the social imperative, is enforced by both.

The coercive operation of external sanctions is of course specially necessary in the case of a citizen of bad disposition. Such a one, moreover, will be restrained from wrongdoing mainly by the apprehension of the punishments incident in a settled community to breaches of the law, whereas the ordinary man will be restrained from transgressions —so far as the restraint is external—almost entirely by the apprehension of social disapproval and its inevitable manifestations.

Now, whatever be the precise scope of a particular sanction, and whether it be legal or social, its essential characteristic is that it is a *probability*, rather than a certainty, of evil consequences in the case of wrongdoing. To take one illustration, manslaughter is prohibited by the law of this country. The sanction of this prohibition is any term of incarceration up to that involved by a life sentence. A man may commit what is in fact a grave case of this crime. But the crime itself may not be detected ; or the offender may escape ; or those who are cognizant of the circumstances may neither prosecute him nor give information to the police authorities ; or, upon a trial, justice may miscarry altogether, or the punishment may be only nominal.

Similarly, a man may be guilty of conduct of a kind which, although not criminal, is regarded by the community as disgraceful. But the offence may remain secret, or those who discover it may not expose the offender, or for some other reason he may escape serious animadversion upon his conduct. The degree of uncertainty as to the actual infliction of the evil in question need not, however, necessarily be greater in the case of a social sanction than in that of a sanction of the law. In both cases alike the restraining power—the real sanction—is the *probability* of evil only. The fact that the evil if suffered at all will in the one case be inflicted by functionaries of the state, and in the other by persons who cannot be precisely determined beforehand, distinguishes the two classes of sanctions; but it is well that the importance of this distinction, substantial as it is, should not be over-estimated.

In a modern state, under normal conditions, offences which are generally regarded as grave are, for the most part, prohibited by the criminal law, and this is administered in a way which satisfies the public feeling against criminals. Spontaneous intervention on the part of ordinary citizens in the infliction of punishment in such cases is wholly unnecessary. Any such intervention indeed would in itself amount to an assertion of an authority in rivalry to that of the established government and constitute disorderly and insubordinate conduct. Under these circumstances legal sanctions are in practice so clearly distinguished from social sanctions that their essential similarity is concealed.

But in any community where the Courts of Law fail to punish offenders to the satisfaction of the public it is different. If, through the delays and uncertainties of legal procedure, or the weakness of the central government, or the fact that the reign of law has not been fully established, society feels that it is not adequately protected by legal sanctions, it tends to take the punishment of transgressors into its own hands in comparatively irregular ways. The essential resemblance on the part of social sanctions to the sanctions of law is then more obvious. Indeed, we may say generally that, in so far as in any human society offences are not repressed by the means of state authority and law, there is a tendency on the part of the members of the community to protect themselves by other means and for social sanctions to assume in practice, as well as in principle, a close resemblance to the sanctions of law.

It appears, then, that the sanctions which are necessary for the protection of society as it now exists consist of the probability of evil to be incurred by those who offend its collective will. It has now to be noted that this probability rests upon the Force of the community. Unless the offender be for practical purposes weaker than those whose will he has contravened—unless as it were he is in a minority—he cannot have offended any true law or the social imperative. No real sanction could have existed to restrain his action, nor indeed could any social sense have willed the contrary.

And even though in a law-abiding state the social sanction may for the most part take the form of a mere manifestation of general disapproval, it none the less rests upon Force. The disapproval owes its deterrent character—its effectiveness as a sanction—to the fact that it is really irresistible and in the last resort may become overwhelming.

Accordingly, it may be said that it is essential to the good order of any community that certain rules of conduct and administrative ordinances should be supported by a sanction consisting of a probability that those who transgress them will suffer evil at the hands of the community through some of its members acting either *de jure* or *de facto* on its behalf. The true function of force in the regulation of conduct is the provision of the means of creating this standing probability. And the probability that a society will exercise its inherent force upon appropriate occasions may be sufficient to constitute an effective sanction although it may not be wielded by a sovereign authority or in accordance with positive law.

This sanction is necessary to the maintenance of order not only in any society of individuals but also in the great society of states.

The question thus arises whether the society of states can provide this sanction. Can they make such arrangements as will establish a standing probability that any state which violently opposes the general welfare will be overcome and punished by the might of other states ?

Latent in the society of states there must necessarily be the force sufficient to inflict evil upon a state which opposes the general will. And inasmuch as there is no established sovereign authority over this society, there is nothing to render the infliction of such evil by the spontaneous action of particular states improper or unnecessary. Up to the present time, however, the probability that this force would be exerted in an appropriate case has not existed, or, at all events, has not been sufficiently strong to prevent the outbreak of aggressive wars.

Such a probability will be practically established only if means are devised whereby this force may be set in motion and brought to bear effectively against disturbers of the peace.

PROPOSITION XI.—The proper function of force in the regulation of conduct is the provision of a standing probability that violent opposition to the general will of a society will be restrained or punished; and the force of any society is necessarily adequate for this purpose.

8

CHAPTER XII

INTERNATIONAL LAW

THE operation of general rules in maintaining order is limited by the extent to which the process of social integration has proceeded among those to whom they are addressed. And this process can be inchoate only in any aggregate so long as the bulk of the individuals lack homogeneity in character and their mutual relations are intermittent or unstable.

Owing to the great diversities between the various races of mankind; the limited and imperfect intercourse between them; the absence of any universal and comprehensive social sense or community of sentiment; the constant changes in the absolute and relative composition and strength of states; the instability of their relations with one another; and the dynamic character of their existence: the world regarded as a whole has—at all events until quite recently—continued in a rudimentary condition of social organization and cohesion. Naturally, therefore, there have always been grave difficulties in the way of the effective regulation of the conduct of states by general rules; and it is by no means a matter for surprise that their behaviour to one another has never hitherto been consistent with the maintenance of general order.

It is, however, the fact that a body of rules and

principles is in existence which is generally supposed among civilized men to be binding upon states in their mutual relations. The nature and content of these rules and principles we must now consider critically. We shall then be in a position to judge how far they satisfy the need of a standard of public right and how far they leave room for the necessity of administrative action in the regulation of the conduct of states.

International Law is a subject which is always of immediate practical importance. Yet it is extremely difficult to gain a just conception of its nature and provisions or to form a reasonable estimate of the extent to which it influences the conduct of mankind.

It is easy to distinguish International Law from Positive Law or Law as it prevails in any particular state. Positive Law consists of rules of conduct binding upon the citizens of a state and enforced by the supreme authority therein. Its distinctive characteristic is the definite sanction by which the authority of the rule is supported—the probability that its violation will be followed by a coercive order made by a tribunal of the state and carried into effect, where necessary, by executive officers. On the other hand, International Law has not hitherto been systematically enforced by any supreme authority. It postulates, indeed, that no such authority exists. It is not supported at present by any sanction beyond the probability that a clear and important breach of its provisions committed without any extenuating circumstances would be generally disapproved throughout the society of states. The possibility of war has never

up to the present time constituted a true sanction :
for a standing probability that the aggressive state
would be defeated has not hitherto been established.

International Law, said Professor Holland,
' differs from ordinary law in being unsupported by
the authority of a state. It differs from ordinary
morality in being a rule for states and not for individuals. It is the vanishing point of Jurisprudence ; since it lacks any arbiter of disputed
questions, save public opinion, beyond and above
the disputant parties themselves, and since, in
proportion as it tends to become assimilated to
true law by the aggregation of states into a larger
society, it ceases to be itself, and is transmuted
into the public law of a federal government. The
realization of the " *civitas maxima* " of which
theorists have dreamed would thus be not the
triumph but the extinction of International Law,
which can subsist only between states which, on the
one hand, sufficiently resemble one another, and are
closely enough knit together by common interests
to be susceptible of a uniform pressure of public
opinion, while, on the other hand, they are not so
politically combined as to be controlled by the
force of a central authority.' [1]

For reasons, however, which have already been
partly indicated and which will be more fully
considered hereafter, the perception of the fact—

[1] *Jurisprudence*, 13th ed. pp. 391–2. It is to be observed that
the designation of the system as ' International Law,' which
was introduced by Bentham, is in itself somewhat unfortunate.
The system applies between states, and not between nations,
and can be called ' law ' only by a very extended use of this
word.

important as it is—that International Law has hitherto not been supported by an adequate sanction, should not in itself lead us to depreciate the actual, or still less the potential, value of the system.

But, when we turn to the positive side of the subject, great care is necessary in order to keep on anything like firm ground. What is International Law ? what are its provisions ? and how far do they consist of operative rules which really regulate the conduct of states ?

In the first place it is necessary to observe that International Law, to use the terminology of Grotius, is the *Jus Belli ac Pacis*. No one could read the work of this great man without perceiving that it is mainly a treatise on war. And, indeed, by far the greater part of the definite rules which are comprised in the system at the present day are concerned with the conduct of war as between one belligerent and another and as between the belligerents and neutrals. The value of these rules need not be considered here. Inasmuch as, in this treatise, we are concerned with the preservation of peace—the primary object of rules of conduct—they are irrelevant to our purpose.

The present inquiry is then limited to the *Jus Pacis*. What is the International Law of Peace ?

In a judgment of the Judicial Committee of the Privy Council, delivered by Lord Parker of Waddington, it was said that International Law ' originates in the practice and usage long observed by civilized nations in their relations towards each other or in express international agreement.' [1]

[1] The Zamora, Law Reports [1916], 2 A.C. 77 at p. 91.

If in this sentence the word 'nations' be understood to mean states, it may be accepted as a compendious indication of the nature of that part of the system, called by jurists International Law, which consists of definite rules of real validity—that is to say, rules the provisions of which can be stated clearly and the obligatory character of which is the subject of general recognition.

For many centuries, speaking generally, every civilized man has owned allegiance to some particular community called a state. Each state has exercised control throughout a definite land area, and states with sea-coasts have asserted their authority over the adjacent waters. The citizens of the several European states have to a greater or less extent respectively traded with the citizens of other states, and visited their territories. The governments of the various states have maintained intercourse with one another by accredited diplomatic agents and also by the occasional exchange of visits between their sovereigns or chief rulers and ships of war or other armed forces.

In other words, each state has exercised control over its natural born subjects within its own territory, and has also recognized them as its citizens wherever they might for the time being chance to be. It has also exercised a temporary jurisdiction over ordinary foreigners while they were within its own borders or the waters adjacent thereto. But the several governments have received one another's agents on the footing that they should be treated in such a way as to render the due discharge of their representative functions practicable. They have also received sovereigns, ships of war, and other armed forces, on the understanding that their distinctive characters should be respectively observed.

These fundamental conditions of the actual life of Europe have been recognized by jurists ; and their necessary implications form the substratum of the International Law of Peace. The fact that a particular government exercises control over a particular area, without habitual interference on the part of any other government, entitles it, in the view of the jurist, to continue to exercise such authority. The actual status is clothed with a jural character. So long as it endures, the implications of supreme rights and jurisdiction follow.

The fact of control, which in the case of land forms a clear and definite basis for the jural conception of sovereignty, and the usages naturally arising out of possession, do not, however, exist in the same way with regard to the parts of the globe which are covered by water. On the one hand, the high seas are not susceptible of appropriation ; while, on the other, the waters adjacent to land, to undefined limits, are susceptible of control, and the exercise of this is essential in the interests of the bordering states. Moreover, intercourse between states involves the passage into the territorial waters of one state of ships containing organized parties of the citizens of other states. From these circumstances there obviously arises the necessity for some usages regulating the respective rights of states with regard to the seas, but the extent of the necessary rights is not indicated by the fundamental facts of the case with the same certainty as in the case of the land. Accordingly, we find that international usages with regard to the seas, while by no means devoid of authority, are largely wanting in precision.

The true character and degree of acceptance of the usages in this connexion are well shown in the following passages from the work of the late Mr. W. E. Hall on *International Law* : [1]

' In claiming its marginal seas as property a state is able to satisfy the condition of valid appropriation, because a narrow belt of water along a coast can be effectively commanded from the coast itself either by guns or by means of a coastguard. . . . On the assumption that any part of the sea is susceptible of appropriation, no serious question can arise as to the existence of property in marginal waters.   Their precise extent, however, is not so certain.   Generally their limit is fixed at a marine league from the shore ; but . . . perhaps it may be said without impropriety that a state has theoretically the right to extend its territorial waters from time to time at its will with the increased range of guns. . . . In any case the custom of regarding a line three miles from land as defining the boundary of marginal territorial waters is so far fixed that a state must be supposed to accept it in the absence of express notice that a larger extent is claimed.

' It seems to be generally thought that straits are subject to the same rule as the open sea. . . . This doctrine, however, is scarcely consistent with the view, which is also generally taken, that gulfs of a greater or less size in the opinion of different writers, when running into the territory of a single state, can be included within its territorial waters ; perhaps also it is not in harmony with the actual

[1] 8th ed. pp. 190–7.

practice with respect to waters of the latter kind.
. . . In principle it is difficult to separate gulfs and
straits from one another. . . . On the whole question
it is scarcely possible to say anything more definite
than that, while on the one hand it may be doubted
whether any state would now seriously assert a
right of property over broad straits or gulfs of considerable size and wide entrance, there is on the
other hand nothing in the conditions of valid maritime occupation to prevent the establishment of a
claim either to basins of considerable area, if approached by narrow entrances such as those of the
Zuyder Zee, or to large gulfs which, in proportion
to the width of their mouth, run deeply into the
land, even when so large as Delaware Bay, or still
more to small bays, such as that of Cancale.

' In all cases in which territorial waters are
so placed that passage over them is either necessary
or convenient for the navigation of open seas, as
in that of marginal waters, or of an appropriated
strait connecting unappropriated waters, they are
subject to a right of innocent use by all mankind
for the purposes of commercial navigation.'

Again, the fact that intercourse between states
has been maintained by agents who, in order that
the objects of their mission should be conveniently
and completely achieved, have necessarily been
treated on a special footing, has involved the growth
of definite usages as to their immunity from the
jurisdiction of the states to which they are accredited.
These usages constitute one of the largest and most
authoritative departments of the international
system. If, indeed, we read such a chapter as that
of Mr. Hall on ' Sovereignty in Relation to the

Territory of the State ' we find that, for the greater part, it is concerned with a discussion of the immunities of the sovereigns, diplomatic agents, and armed forces of foreign states.   Here also we perceive that International Law has actuality.   It consists of propositions which naturally follow from existing states of fact, and which are supported by definite usages which have long been very generally and continuously observed.   It is especially noteworthy in this connexion that, even during the Great War, the immunities of diplomatic agents were for the most part respected by all the belligerents.

The intercourse between states has also naturally given rise from time immemorial to express agreements between them.   The disposition to make contracts is universal in social human nature.   The making of any kind of agreement necessarily involves the assumption on the part of both parties that its provisions ought to be observed.   This necessary assumption is recognized by International Law ; and much has been written by jurists upon the subject of treaties.   But all that is of real validity in this connexion may probably be correctly summarized in the statement that *the provisions of a duly concluded treaty ought to be observed according to their true meaning and intent*.   Treaties will occasionally be violated until human nature becomes perfect.   But the principle of their obligatory effect is immutably founded in the social nature of mankind.

It is thus apparent that the system known as International Law consists, to a considerable extent, of usages which have naturally and necessarily arisen out of the salient facts of state existence and the intercourse which has taken place between the governments of states and between the citizens of the various states respectively and the citizens of other states. So far as Europe, or the world, has maintained general social relations—so far as a genuine European or world-wide society or social life has existed—usages to regulate these relations and social life have been necessary. Such usages have accordingly been evolved naturally, and they have constituted a system which in the main has fulfilled its proper function. To this extent International Law is the recognition and expression of the jural consequences of the realities of the existence of states and of the relations between their governments and between the government of one state and the citizens of another. It is a body of customary rules of practical utility and real authority ; and there is a general assumption on the part of civilized mankind that these rules will be observed, as in fact they generally are.

But a glance at the table of contents of any standard work on International Law, still confining our attention to the rules of peace, will make it clear that writers upon the subject do not by any means limit it to usages such as we have been considering. In their view the system largely consists of rules of the Roman Civil Law applied to the regulation of the relations of states *inter se*. In other words, certain rules which arose out of the relations of individuals as citizens of a particular state have been declared by jurists to be binding upon the governments of states. It follows that these rules have not been naturally evolved from the existence of states and the relations between them or their citizens.

They have in fact been artificially imported into the discussion of controversies which from time to time have arisen between states by the ratiocinative skill of legal experts.

States have from time to time founded colonies in territories unoccupied by civilized races. Successive occupations by different states on the same continent have naturally led to disputes as to boundaries. The statesmen of the rival powers have called in the assistance of lawyers. The lawyers have almost inevitably conducted their arguments upon the basis that rules of the legal system with which they were all alike familiar were properly applicable to the matters in hand. Accordingly, agreements and arbitral awards concerning the acquisition and retention of territory have commonly proceeded upon the assumption that the rules of the Civil Law as to title by *occupatio* and *accessio* were binding between states. In a sense, therefore, it may be said that these rules are part of the International system.

But a close examination of the classic cases of disputes as to title to territory reveals the difficulties inherent in the application of rules regulating private ownership to rival interstatal claims to vast tracts of newly discovered continents. Too often, indeed, the attempted presentation of the supposed rule by writers on International Law is little more than a narrative of successive quarrels and unadmitted claims, which leave it by no means clear whether any particular recorded case is properly to be regarded as a precedent tending to establish a general rule or as an illustration of conduct which is to be deemed illegal.

Accordingly, when it is considered how inadequate the rules in question really are for the purpose in view, how often they have been disregarded or evaded, and how little has been the effect which they have had in determining the conduct of states, until after critical quarrels have arisen, it would be misleading to attribute to them an efficacy like that of the usages to which we have referred above.

The civil law of Rome, it must be remembered, consists entirely of law adapted to the requirements of a settled community of individuals—a community which has reached a stable form. And International Law, at the same time that it purports to adopt the principles of this system of jurisprudence, assumes that the *status quo* in respect of the territorial possessions of states is legally immutable. It has, however, been pointed out in Chapter II that, although statesmen as well as lawyers habitually express themselves as if political geography were permanent, it is in fact constantly changing. Moreover, even at the present time, the states of the world considered collectively constitute only a rudimentary social organism. Many years must pass away before they develop into a true community and acquire a stable social structure. Meanwhile, much will be necessary for the effective adjustment of the relations of states which is altogether outside the scope of Roman jurisprudence.

We pass now to consider a third aspect of International Law.

As presented by Grotius and the text-writers who have followed him the system consists, not only of the usages of states and the rules of the *Corpus Juris Civilis* which have already been considered, but also of the provisions of the Law of Nature so far as it is applicable to the relations of states.

From very remote times it must have been observed that the normal civilized man has a faculty of perceiving a difference between right and wrong and of forming moral judgments accordingly. It is therefore easy to understand why many philosophers during the last three thousand years have adopted the hypothesis of a Law of Nature. The conception of a universally obligatory Law, the dictates of which are assumed to be the appropriate objects of the apprehension of the conscience, is the logical complement of the conception of a moral sense. ' Moral duty was by ' the Stoics ' practically deduced from, or identified with, the Law of Nature.' [1]

The theory of the Law of Nature has, however, usually been more or less associated with conceptions which are not essentially connected with the moral sense of mankind. By an easy and obvious transition of thought it was supposed that this Law prevailed at the remote period of the infancy of the human race, when men were living in a state of nature ; and, accordingly, that its provisions were obligatory upon rational creatures whenever they were not associated together in a common civil allegiance.

If the writers on the ' Law of Nations ' had adopted the theory of the Law of Nature merely as the hypothesis of the principles communicated by Nature to the soul of man, and had been content with the proposition that a state is substantially

[1] Bryce's *Studies in History and Jurisprudence*, vol. ii. p. 137.

and practically, as well as by analogy, a moral entity, and therefore subject to the obligations which are incumbent upon the consciences of individual men, they would have enunciated in a convenient and unobjectionable form a truth of fundamental importance, upon which even at the present day it is still necessary to insist. Instead of this they directed their attention to the conception of the Law of Nature as the system of principles assumed to have been applicable to the relations of men while living in a state of nature. They then proceeded to argue that, as states were not themselves subject to any common sovereignty, they were *inter se* in a state of nature, and accordingly that the Law of Nature in this secondary meaning must be obligatory upon them.

The theory of a Law of Nature adopted in this sense has been a fertile source of illusion and confusion. Any law, even though it be identified with the dictates of conscience or of the supreme authority over man, by whatever name it may be called, so far as it purports to regulate the relations between human beings, presupposes their social nature. The development of rules of conduct can proceed only *pari passu* with the development of society. Any rules or principles which apply to the relations of either individuals or states must depend for their obligatory effect upon the existence of social conditions, however rudimentary they may in fact be.

Accordingly, when International Law, as expounded by the jurists, proceeds to enunciate the logical consequences of the fallacious doctrine that states as between themselves are in a state of nature, it parts company with reality and utility. It propounds the dogmas of the independence of every separate state and of the equality of all states with one another. These dogmas are open to objection not only, or indeed mainly, because they do not correspond with existing facts. They could not be accepted in practice without destroying all reasonable hope of the prevention of war, or indeed without undermining such social order as now prevails throughout the world.

Good sense and the demands of practical utility arising from the common interests of states have proved far too strong for the jurists in this connexion. In so far as the system of International Law is to be taken as incorporating these supposed deductions from an imaginary law—a law which could never have prevailed at all under the circumstances assumed—it has always been more honoured in the breach than the observance. It differs *in toto* from the other departments of the system with which we have dealt. It is not based on inveterate usage ; nor does it rest upon an analogical extension of the rules of a body of jurisprudence which is generally recognized as a guide to the decision of cases which are not covered by any local law. It has indeed no real validity whatever.

' No principles,' said Dr. Lorimer, writing in 1883,[1] ' have been repeated more frequently or authoritatively than the equality of states and their absolute independence, except perhaps their counterparts, the balance of powers and the *status quo* ; and all of them may now, I think, be safely

[1] *Law of Nations*, vol. i. p. 44.

said to have been repudiated by history, as they always were by reason.'

If the reader were now to turn to any well-known book on International Law, he would perceive that, in what has been said in this chapter, we have in effect briefly indicated and reviewed the principal provisions of that part of the system which consists of the rules of peace.

The resulting conclusion appears to be this. International Law, in so far as it propounds as general principles the necessary implications of the separate political existence of states and incorporates the inveterate usages prevailing between the governments of states and between the government of one state and the citizens of others, is of indubitable and permanent value. So far as it purports to go further, its validity is more or less open to question. In indicating a standard of legal principles, to which, in cases of dispute, statesmen can appeal as plausible alternatives to forcible means of decision, it has, to an extent which it would be difficult to gauge, proved from time to time of great practical utility. It has also been of service in contributing to the development of the conception that a state is a moral entity and bound to comport itself accordingly. But, in so far as it has been committed to vague generalizations deduced from an imaginary Law of Nature serious obstacles have been raised to its own progressive development.

It follows that no one who has a just and comprehensive conception of International Law should feel any surprise that it has not proved an effective means of preventing wars.

9

In the future the utility of the system will no doubt be greatly enhanced in many respects by international conventions, and the jurisprudence of the Permanent Court of International Justice which will give a more definite character to certain of its provisions. But in this connexion it should not be forgotten that every rule is in a sense a limitation of liberty and only to be justified by its practical utility. Unless a rule is from its nature likely to be observed in critical cases by all the states concerned it may well prove in its general result predominantly mischievous.

For the rest, the salient truth is this. If everything possible were accomplished for the improvement of International Law—even indeed if an adequate sanction for its provisions were provided —it would still in itself be a wholly insufficient means of maintaining the general peace. Without effective international administration the affairs of the society of states cannot be properly regulated, and a rigid system of general rules might work more harm than good.

PROPOSITION XII.—The system known as International Law, even if reinforced by an effective sanction, would be an inadequate basis of public right.

CHAPTER XIII

THE INTERDEPENDENCE OF STATES

NO society could exist as an organized community in which all the members should be independent. Every social union restrains or qualifies the independence of the associated members. To the extent indeed to which a number of individuals are associated together—to the extent to which they form an organized society —their several independence is forgone.

The true object of a state, as of every other social union, is the enlargement of the freedom of the individual members or their power of realizing their respective wills. This greater freedom of action on the part of the citizens can be achieved only by the exclusion of their independence. Independence is an anti-social conception. It connotes anarchy. Man by virtue of his membership of a civilized community obtains real and substantial liberty at the price of exclusion from the illusive independence of a solitary savage.

' Freedom and independence, though so often confounded, are so far from being identical, that, in human relations, they are not even reconcilable.'[1]

No social organism, moreover, can be evolved without the development of inequalities as between the individual members. The progressive growth

[1] Lorimer's *Law of Nations*, vol. i. p. 2.

of any living organism involves the differentiation of its functions. If it were possible for any nation to persist in maintaining a condition of absolute equality as between all its members individually, such a nation could never become a state. The development of a community of men into a state or political society involves the recognition of inequalities between the members. The establishment of order necessitates relations of superiority and inferiority.

Social order implies, of course, the existence of a society. General rules of conduct can prevail only in proportion to the degree in which those who are to be affected by them approximate to an organized social community.

The influence of International Law can be established firmly only by developing the social relations of states. Only to the extent to which the world evolves the essential characteristics of a social organism can peace be established on a firm and lasting foundation. The society of states must become an active reality before social order can be maintained permanently throughout the world.

When, therefore, the professors of International Law declare that one of its postulates is the independence and equality of states they advance a proposition which is fundamentally inconsistent with the practical development of the system. At the same time they raise the most formidable difficulties in the way of efficient international administration.

Every one recognizes the fact that, normally but to an undefined extent, it is best that separate states, like separate individuals, should manage their own affairs. The problem of the future is this—how is the autonomy of states—their practical independence with regard to internal government—to be reconciled with the well-being of the world at large considered as a great society of states ? How is the supremacy of states with regard to their internal affairs to be rendered consistent with the interdependence of states as regards the general welfare ?

Let us in the first place attempt to form a clear conception of the real position of states in relation to one another.

The world is tending to become as a whole a true society. With the general intellectual and moral advancement of mankind, the improvement of communications between the various peoples, the general diffusion of information upon contemporary events, and the consequent growth of an international public opinion, a real world-society is being gradually evolved. We have seen that, for an indefinite period of the future, the formation of a universal state cannot reasonably be anticipated. But a sense of human solidarity is steadily developing. Already throughout a very large proportion of mankind there is sufficient community of sentiment to form a basis for satisfactory social relations. As between several great nations, indeed, there is now sufficient sympathy and moral similarity to render joint action on their part possible even in long-sustained measures of far-reaching significance. And on the part of the more advanced communities there appears to be a rapidly growing disposition to grapple with the affairs of the world as a whole. Already the process of social integration has probably gone farther than is generally realized ; and it seems evident that the elements of cohesion have for some time been, and still are, in a condition of special activity. It would be unfortunate if statesmen, even with the best intentions, were to retard this beneficent process by attempting to insist upon conditions of state existence which are the negation of social order.

Owing to the rudimentary social cohesion which already exists between the various states they cannot all be independent in fact.

It may, however, be said that each of the Great Powers is, in the ordinary meaning of the words, practically independent. Its absolute strength is great. Its relative strength at any particular time is ascertainable only by war. If attacked, the possibility of combination with other states has had to be taken into account. In the result, no Power has been the subject of the direct interference in its affairs of other states, except where war on a vast scale was deliberately contemplated. Accordingly, every Power, so long as it refrains from doing anything which would excite the active hostility of another Power, is free to do what it pleases. As a matter of practical politics, therefore, good reasons have hitherto existed for the conventional assumption that the Great Powers are respectively independent. These states have, in fact, acquired collectively a distinctive position as a rudimentary world-organ of direction and control.

Side by side with these Great Powers there exist a large number of smaller states. Most of these relatively to the Great Powers have practically hardly any power at all. Their separate existence is not dependent primarily upon their own strength. In each case it is due to other causes. *A fortiori* these states cannot maintain the peace of the world outside their own borders. They are not in fact independent, nor can they maintain the independence of other states.

A little state indeed enjoys its separate existence at the inevitable cost of exclusion from direct and substantial authority in the affairs of the world at large.

If we turn to the legal aspect of the matter we are confronted not only with the principle that law, in the strict sense of the term, is inconsistent with independence, but also with the fact that as between states it is conceded that no such law exists. Moreover, with regard to what is called ' International Law,' we have seen that usage does not recognize the independence of small states. On the contrary, the habitual conduct of the Great Powers with regard to them is inconsistent with any assumption of such independence.

Can it then be maintained that, as a matter of right or morals, every little state ought to be independent ? or rather, that, by common consent, it should be treated as if it were independent ?

Every community which is organized as a political entity ; which possesses a defined territory ; and which manages its own affairs apart from any external control regularly exercised over it by any other particular community, is a state. As such it is entitled, according to the general view of mankind and what appears to be the essential justice of the matter, to freedom of action, so far as this is consistent with the welfare of other states. But the attempt to assure to every state absolute independence would hinder the development of the social organization of the world as a whole which is a necessary condition of the maintenance of general order and the permanent preservation of peace.

The theory of the equality of all states rests upon no better foundation either of fact or principle than that of their independence.

' All states are equally entitled to be recognized as states, on the simple ground that they are states ; but all states are not entitled to be recognized as equal states, simply because they are not equal states.' [1]   Any attempt to establish an artificial equality must tend in the long run to the aggravation, rather than to the mitigation, of the inequality which exists in fact.

The prevalence of this dogma of equality, like that of independence, seriously obscures the essential features of the real position occupied by the smaller states and the conditions upon which their tenure of separate existence has long depended ; and may also prove an obstacle in the way of the future developments by which alone their interests can be adequately secured.

Writers on International Law have, indeed, recently manifested an increasingly decided disposition to take this view of the dogmas in question.

' The equality of sovereign states,' said Dr. Westlake,[2] ' is merely their independence under a different name.   We are here irresistibly reminded

---

[1] Lorimer's *Law of Nations*, vol. ii. p. 260, note.
[2] *International Law*, pt. i., ' Peace,' pp. 321–3.

of the existence in Europe of the great powers as a separate and recognized class, and are led to ask whether it can be reconciled with the equality and independence which international law deems to belong to the smaller powers. . . . We are in presence of the first stages of a process which in the course of ages may lead to organized government among states, as the indispensable condition of their peace. . . . The world in which the largest intercourse of civilized men has been from time to time carried on has not always been distributed into equal and independent states, and we are reminded by what we see that it may not always continue to be so distributed.'

Similarly but more emphatically Dr. T. J. Lawrence says : ' An examination of modern international history reveals a number of facts which it is hard to reconcile with the old theory of the complete equality of all fully sovereign states. They seem instead to point to a primacy on the part of the foremost powers of the civilized world.' [1] ' Attempts are made to reconcile them with the doctrine of the equality of all sovereign states by pointing out that what they establish is a political inequality, whereas what the old theory asserted was a legal equality. It is a grave question whether the legal and the political aspects of the problem can be parted and kept separate in this way. . . . In a system of rules depending, like International Law, for their validity on general consent, what is political is legal also, if it is generally accepted and acted on.' [2] ' There is no moral

[1] *Principles of International Law*, 7th ed. p. 245.
[2] *Ibid.* p. 252.

or jural necessity about the doctrine of equality. The society of nations has changed its form in the past, and there is nothing inherently improbable in the idea that it is experiencing another change in our own time. It may be working round again to the old notion of a common superior—not indeed a pope or an emperor, but a committee, or body of representatives from its leading states. If this is the real explanation of the phenomena . . . probably the new organization will be world-wide rather than European, and the Great Powers of the future will be the leading members of the society of nations without regard to geographical situation.' [1]

In short, the theories of the independence and equality of all states are inconsistent with the principles of the evolution of a world-society ; and any efforts to insist upon their application in practice would accordingly tend to impede the development of the conditions which are necessary to the establishment of peace.

PROPOSITION XIII.—The process of coalescence whereby the world is developing into a social community involves inequalities between the several states and excludes the possibility of the complete independence of all.

[1] *Principles of International Law*, 7th ed. pp. 253-4.

CHAPTER XIV

THE PASSING OF NEUTRALITY [1]

IN order that the conduct of states may be effectively regulated and the peace of the world as far as possible assured, three things are necessary :

1. A considerable development of the general will of the society of states as a collective whole—a development resulting not only in well-defined and universally accepted customs and conventional rules, but a genuine international social imperative and a vigorous, alert, and articulate public opinion.

2. The establishment of an administrative authority capable of dealing *ad hoc* with particular difficulties arising in the society of states which do not admit of solution by the application of any generally accepted rule.

3. The constitution of a standing probability that a state which disturbs the peace by acting in violent contravention of the general will of the society of states will suffer evil consequences at the hands of some power or powers acting on their behalf.

[1] In view of the present attitude of opinion with regard to Neutrality, it may be of interest to point out that this chapter, with the exception of the passage between brackets on pp. 143-4, reproduces literally the text of the corresponding chapter, entitled ' The Duty of Intervention,' in the edition of this book published in April 1918.

We have now to deal specifically with the third of these conditions. In order that this may be attained it is necessary that there should be on the part of the states of goodwill and their peoples a realization and recognition of their joint and several responsibility for the preservation of the general order and of the consequent duty incumbent upon them all alike of doing everything in their power to prevent any state or states from waging an unjust and aggressive war. Unless it be reasonably certain that, if any particular community be attacked, others will be ready to take active parts in the war against the aggressor, there can be no standing probability that a delinquent state will be defeated in its object or punished for its conduct.

Hitherto no such duty has been generally recognized. The idea indeed of every state intervening, or being conditionally bound to intervene, in every war would have been almost inconceivable until comparatively recent times. And even now there will be many minds which will honestly and intelligently arrive at the conviction that, when war occurs, the great desideratum must be to limit the area of hostilities, and that, on the whole, the general interests will be best served by each state confining its active operations to matters which are its own direct and immediate concern. Moreover, quite apart from the conclusions of reason there will be a strong disposition on the part of many states to avoid participation in strife from self-regarding motives, based on considerations of a proximate character, instead of the wider consideration of the general and lasting welfare of the world at large.

It may, however, be contended with great

cogency that the system of International Law in so far as it purports to be obligatory upon states, involves the implication of the suggested duty of intervention. If no state, other than the immediate parties to a controversy, is concerned therein, International Law can have no semblance of a sanction. Unless a breach of the rules of this system casts some obligation upon states which are not directly injured thereby, the system must tend to be regarded rather as a pretence than a reality ; or, perhaps worse still, as an actual restraint upon well-disposed states only, and, therefore, not improbably a disadvantage to them in their relations to other states.

The germ of the conception of the several and collective responsibility of states for forming a judgment upon the merits of a particular dispute and acting accordingly is really to be found in the treatise of Grotius himself.

' It is,' says he, ' the duty of neutrals to do nothing which may strengthen the side which has the worse cause, or which may impede the motions of him who is carrying on a just war . . . and in a doubtful case to act alike to both sides in permitting transit, in supplying provisions, in not helping persons besieged.' [1] And speaking of the supply by a neutral to an enemy of objects of ambiguous use, after saying that the state of the war is to be considered, Grotius adds : ' If, besides, the injustice of my enemy to me be very evident, and he ' (the neutral) ' confirm him in a most unjust war, he will then be bound to me not only civilly for the

[1] *De Jure Belli et Pacis*, Whewell's translation, bk. iii. cap. xvii. sect. iii. 1.

damage, but also criminally as being one who protects a manifest criminal from the judge who is about to inflict punishment.' [1]

After the time of Grotius, however, jurists and statesmen elaborated the doctrines of neutrality in such a way and to such an extent as to undermine, and indeed very largely to destroy, the authority of the international system. While ingeniously developing the supposed implications of neutrality, they overlooked the cardinal implication of any system of International Law that neutrality is not normally a moral attitude.

The obligations of neutrality, as set forth by the writers on the subject, are, it is to be observed, the obligations of a state which wishes to keep out of a war towards the actual belligerents. The obligation with which we are now concerned is the obligation of every state to the society of states as a whole. If such an obligation exists it must obviously transcend all others.

The narrow and self-regarding view of neutrality was prominently enunciated by Bynkershoek in 1737. The duty of neutrals, he said, ' is to use all care not to meddle in the war. . . . If I am neutral, I cannot give an advantage to one party, lest I injure the other. . . . It is more essential to remain in amity with both than to favour the hostilities of one and so make a tacit renunciation of the friendship of the other.' Even this writer, however, had some conception of the higher aspect of the matter. When, for example, he discusses the posi-

---

[1] *De Jure Belli et Pacis*, Whewell's translation, bk. iii. cap. i. sect. v. 3. See also bk. i. cap. v. sect. ii. ; bk. ii. cap. xv. 13 ; bk. ii. cap. xx. sect. xl. ; bk. ii. cap. xxv. sect. vi.

tion of a neutral who is under an obligation by treaty to furnish help to one who has afterwards become a belligerent, he says that the neutral may abstain from rendering the promised assistance where the war has been undertaken unjustly on the part of the state to which it had been promised.[1]

The United States of America did much to develop and elaborate the body of usages and rules based upon the supposed duty of neutrals to abstain from acts calculated to assist either of the parties to a war. Their policy in 1793 constituted ' an epoch in the development of the usages of neutrality. There can be no doubt that it was intended and believed to give effect to the obligations then incumbent upon neutrals. But it represented by far the most advanced existing opinions as to what those obligations were ; and in some points it even went further than authoritative international custom ' had advanced up to the time of the Great War.[2]

The traditional policy of the Republic in regard to this subject no doubt accounts very largely for its attitude during this war until the spring of 1917. But by the declaration of hostility which it then made against Germany the last serious obstacle to the development of a sound international system was removed.

[On the 8th August 1932 Mr. H. L. Stimson, who was then the Secretary of State of the Republic, referring to the Briand-Kellogg Treaty, said : ' Consultation between the signatories of the Pact when faced with the threat of its violation, becomes inevitable. . . . That the American people sub-

[1] *Quæstiones Juris Publici*, bk. i. cap. ix.
[2] See Hall's *International Law*, 8th ed. p. 707.

scribe to this view is made clear by the fact that each of the platforms recently adopted by the two great party conventions at Chicago contains planks endorsing the principle of consultation.' [1]   And on the 22nd May 1932 Mr. Norman Davis, speaking as the representative of the United States, made a still more significant advance.   Addressing the General Committee of the Disarmament Conference, he declared : ' I wish to make it clear that we are ready not only to do our part toward the substantive reduction of armaments, but, if this is effected by general international agreement, we are also prepared to contribute in other ways to the organization of peace.   In particular we are willing to consult with other States in case of a threat to peace, with a view of averting conflict.   Further than that, in the event that the States, in conference, determine that a State has been guilty of a breach of the peace in violation of its international obligations, and take measures against the violator, then, if we concur in the judgment rendered as to the responsible and guilty party, we will refrain from any action tending to defeat such collective effort which the States may thus make to restore peace.']

Henceforth, it is conceived, the importance of the doctrines of neutrality must steadily diminish.

It may well be that, in most of the wars that occurred down to the year 1914, the states which remained ' neutral ' were well advised in maintaining an attitude of impartiality, and also that the rules which were from time to time established with regard to the extent of the obligations of

[1] Speech to the Council of Foreign Relations in New York City.

neutrals to abstain from assisting a belligerent had on the whole a beneficial effect. Until comparatively recent times the difficulty of judging upon which side the greater blame might be düe for the outbreak of war would often have been insuperable. The desirability of restricting the area of strife was, moreover, properly a dominant consideration : for the world at large was so far from being in any sense a real society that the intervention of a third party in a particular war would not usually have borne any perceptible relation to a definite system for the preservation of general order.

The aspect of neutrality is now, however, radically different. The world as a whole has become an inchoate social organism. Its constituent communities are beginning to realize their essential solidarity. The knowledge of one another's affairs is leading to the formation, on the part of men collectively, of an international opinion. The common interests of all are beginning to be appreciated by each. If the peace be broken hereafter it will be natural for the citizens of every state to feel the necessity of forming a moral judgment upon the merits of the case and of shaping their own course accordingly.

The claims of self-regarding prudence, moreover, must henceforth yield to the demands of duty to the society of states at large. The preservation of peace is the common interest of all ; and peace can be preserved permanently only if states which are not immediately concerned in any threatened strife are nevertheless willing to participate therein for the sake of the general welfare. The title to

10

peace can be earned only by the readiness to share in the burden of securing it. The common interest of all is the foundation of a common duty.

Every state ought therefore to be willing to co-operate in the forcible measures necessary for the maintenance of order. It does not necessarily follow that, whenever hostile measures are any-where threatened, the whole world should spring to arms. But, in order to provide an effective sanction to peace, by establishing a standing probability that any attempt to disturb it will be defeated, there must be a general and active recogni-tion of the principle that every state ought to be willing to do its best, according to circumstances, to contribute to the success of the champions of interstatal order. Peace can be established upon firm foundations only in accordance with principles which would exclude the right of any state to maintain an attitude of neutrality in the event of war.

PROPOSITION XIV. — Every state is morally bound to co-operate with other states in maintain-ing public right and preserving the general peace.

CHAPTER XV

INTERNATIONAL ADMINISTRATION

IN every organized society order is preserved and the common well-being of the members maintained by general rules and occasional or particular ordinances. For the most part the general rules are prescribed by custom, law, and the social imperative ; while the occasional or particular commands emanate from administrative authority and public opinion.

Rules, which are the formulation of general principles, cannot cover the whole area of social conduct. Even in the most highly developed state, notwithstanding all the accumulated experience of a thousand years or more of collective life, the action of individuals has from time to time to be constrained by particular commands relating to specific matters. Discretionary administration by means of official orders issued *ad hoc* is the necessary complement of the law and the judicature. And in the earlier stages of social development the area of administration, relatively to that of general rules applying to acts of a class, is probably larger than it is in the case of an advanced community. The relative importance, indeed, of administration, as compared with the enforcement of general rules, may be at its maximum in the earliest stage of social order and diminish as social integration proceeds.

Accordingly the affairs of the world considered as a whole could not be regulated satisfactorily in reliance upon general rules alone. The society of states is still in a rudimentary condition, and the scope for administrative activity in its affairs is therefore correspondingly wide. But, even if the process of social integration had gone much farther than it in fact has, the world of states would still need for its complete regulation the occasional ordinances of administrative authority. Only indeed by such intervention could the outbreak of war from some of the causes indicated in Chapter II be provided against with certainty.

Hitherto this aspect of world politics has never received adequate recognition and attention. It has indeed been thoroughly obscured by the postulates of International Law derived from the imaginary Law of Nature and their logical consequences. The doctrines of the independence and equality of all states involve the correlative doctrine of an obligation incumbent upon every state to abstain from intervention in the affairs of any other. Accordingly, this obligation of non-intervention has been persistently said to be prescribed by International Law. Such an obligation, if it existed, would of course exclude the very conception of the administrative action which we are considering in the present chapter.

In fact, however, intervention by one or more states in the affairs of others has frequently taken place throughout all historical times. The instances indeed of such action are so numerous, and many of them from the moral standpoint are so obviously praiseworthy, that writers on International Law have undertaken the difficult task of attempting to reconcile the recorded facts with their theory by developing an ever-increasing list of categories of exceptions to its assumed general applicability. But, while they still cling tenaciously to the letter of the general theory, one may easily discern in their writings the dawn of the recognition of the true and practical principle.

Thus the late Mr. W. E. Hall, dealing at length with the subject in his treatise on *International Law*, puts forward the following conclusions : ' The grounds upon which intervention has taken place, or upon which it is said with more or less of authority that it is permitted, may be referred to the right of self-preservation, to a right of opposing wrongdoing, to the duty of fulfilling engagements, and to friendship for one of two parties in a state.' [1] ' It is unfortunate that publicists have not laid down broadly and unanimously that no intervention is legal, except for the purpose of self-preservation, unless a breach of the law as between states has taken place, or unless the whole body of civilized states have concurred in authorizing it.' [2] It is not difficult to infer from this statement of the conclusions of a very learned and careful author that no valid rule upon the subject has ever existed. And the germ of the true principle at which he hints in the concluding words of this passage is more fully indicated by him elsewhere in these terms : ' A somewhat wider range of intervention than that

---

[1] *International Law*, 8th ed. pp. 338–9.
[2] *Ibid.* pp. 343–4.

which is possessed by individual states may perhaps be conceded to the body of states, or to some of them acting for the whole in good faith with sufficient warrant.' [1]

And Dr. T. J. Lawrence in his work on *The Principles of International Law* says : ' A doctrine of absolute non-intervention has been put forth as a protest against incessant meddling. If this doctrine means that a state should do nothing but mind its own concerns and never take an interest in the affairs of other states, it is fatal to the idea of a family of nations. If, on the other hand, it means that a state should take an interest in international affairs, and express approval or disapproval of the conduct of its neighbours, but never go beyond moral suasion in its interference, it is foolish. To scatter abroad protests and reproaches, and yet to let it be understood that they will never be backed by force of arms, is the surest way to get them treated with angry contempt. Neither selfish isolation nor undignified remonstrance is the proper attitude for honourable and self-respecting states. They should intervene very sparingly, and only on the clearest grounds of justice and necessity ; but when they do intervene, they should make it clear to all concerned that their voice must be attended to and their wishes carried out.' [2]

When we examine the actual course of modern history we find that intervention of an administrative character has in fact very largely contributed to the maintenance of international order. To speak only of the period since 1815, the Great

[1] *International Law*, 8th ed. p. 347.   [2] 7th ed. pp. 134–5.

Powers have in practice assumed, and to a considerable extent exercised, the authority to regulate the positions of the smaller states. It is sufficient in this connexion to refer, by way of illustration, to the instances of the action of the Powers mentioned in various parts of this treatise, and particularly to the action of the Concert of Europe as stated on pages 82–84 above, and of the United States of America with regard to the affairs of the Central and South American Republics.

It is, indeed, evident that the administrative acts by which the Powers have exercised their authority have in many instances been far more effectual in allaying strife than would have been an insistence in the cases in question upon the application of any principles of International Law.

Action similar in its nature will be necessary in the future. Many cases will occur in which the peace will be threatened in consequence of difficulties arising between particular states, where the mere judicial application of any pre-existing general rule would be either impracticable or ineffective, and where rigid insistence upon the *status quo* would involve evils of the gravest character.

Thus, as we have already seen, from time to time, owing to the effects of the spirit of nationality and the operation of other natural causes, certain readjustments of territorial boundaries and rights of jurisdiction become urgently required. It may be, for example, that the limits of particular states have to be brought into a certain correspondence with national areas ; or the means of access to the sea, or a right of passage over part of a river, have become essential to the proper development of the economic life of a state whose population is rapidly increasing. Hitherto changes necessitated by natural causes such as these have generally been accomplished only at the cost of war.

A code of public right which purports to render all existing territorial arrangements and sovereign powers for ever unalterable except with the consent of the states affected and excludes the application of administrative discretion to the solution of difficulties arising from the causes in question, cannot permanently command the full approval of mankind. Nor could it be upheld by any available sanction. The forces of nature at work among the great families of men must in the long run secure their appropriate results. Accordingly, existing boundaries will be altered and territorial rights will be modified, in ways and upon occasions which cannot now be foreseen in detail, notwithstanding the disapproval and opposition of states which may conceive that their own interests will be prejudiced thereby. And, so long as the possibility that a state may have good grounds for a claim to such an alteration is left entirely unrecognized by the standard of Public Right, there will always be the risk that such claims may provoke inevitable and disastrous strife. More than this, exorbitant ambition and unscrupulous greed will find in this omission the pretext for wholly wanton and unwarranted aggression.

The Code of Public Right must then, it is conceived, be modified so as to recognize the necessity for occasional territorial re-arrangements ; it must admit that circumstances of the kind in question may constitute a valid title ; and it must provide the machinery for effecting the proper change.

A useful analogy is to be found in the laws and systems of procedure of modern states. Within the borders of most civilized countries, speaking generally, individual ownership of land is recognized and protected by the law. Under ordinary circumstances no one may annex or even enter the close of another. But where it is shown that, in the general interest of the inhabitants, it is desirable that any particular piece of land belonging to one of them should be compulsorily taken from him by a local authority or a public company, or that an easement in their favour should be created over it, this may be accomplished by virtue of the joint operation of certain general laws and of particular administrative ordinances.

It is noteworthy, moreover, that the power of dealing with land apart from its owner's consent is continually being extended with the advance of civilization. The rights of the former owner have hitherto been recognized for the most part by the award of adequate, or as some would say excessive, compensation. But, even in this respect, the regard for the individual is diminishing while that for the community is increasing.

Similarly, when the general interest of the society of states—the peace and progress of mankind—requires that a portion of the territory of one state should be transferred to another, or that a right of access to the sea should be obtained by one state over the territory of another, it would seem that the justice and propriety of the change should be recognized by international polity.

The reasons, indeed, for giving effect to the requirements of the common weal are more cogent in the case of the society of states than in that of the citizens of a particular state. Owing to the relative difficulty of restraining a tendency to self-redress on the part of states as compared with that of restraining such a tendency on the part of the citizens of a well-ordered community, it is of more urgent practical importance to avoid reasonable ground for dissatisfaction in the former case than in the latter.

It may well be that a practical difficulty may exist as to the matter of compensation in the circumstances contemplated. On the other hand, there will be a general recognition of the principle that, in any territorial re-arrangements, due regard must be paid to the welfare of all the peoples concerned. It seems, indeed, to be probable that the solution of most territorial questions will in practice be very largely assisted by the general development of democratic institutions and the growth of the feeling that *primâ facie* the inhabitants of any portion of the surface of the globe are entitled to have effect given to their wishes as to the particular political unit in which they are to be comprised.

A greater difficulty arises as to the machinery whereby the rights of the states concerned are to be adjusted. At the present stage of our inquiry it is sufficient to say in this connexion that, whatever is to be the authority on which mankind are to rely for the prevention of war, to that authority a state should be at liberty to apply for an award of the kind suggested.

The practical difficulties which have to be sur-

mounted before such an authority can be satisfactorily constituted are the gravest with which
the statesmen of peace are confronted. To many,
indeed, they will long appear insuperable. Let it
therefore be borne in mind that the substance of
the proposal amounts only to this—that changes of
a kind which have hitherto been effected by occasional Congresses, or by the Concert of Europe,
partially and crudely, and generally only after
much bloodshed and suffering, and which it is
certain must be effected in the future by some means
or other, should be accomplished peaceably, justly,
and with due consideration for those primarily
concerned as well as for the welfare and order of
the society of states at large.

The scope for administrative action is further
considered in Chapter XX.

It is now of great practical importance to recognize the fact that those who have hitherto directed
their attention to the problem of the maintenance
of peace have for the most part placed far too much
reliance upon the possible developments of the
system of International Law and the arbitral or
judicial settlement of disputes in accordance with
its provisions. It is high time that the truth should
be generally appreciated and frankly admitted that
the peace and welfare of the world cannot be maintained without the exercise from time to time of
administrative authority. The organization of the
world as a whole cannot be developed adequately into
a really social structure unless its common interests
are the subject of a control which is collective in its
nature. The theory of the absolute independence of
all states and the corollary of the duty of non-inter-

vention are inconsistent with the principles of social order and must accordingly be rejected.

This being so, it follows that it is necessary that there should be a universally recognized authority in every way qualified to act on behalf of the society of states as a whole, and always available when the need for its intervention may arise.

In this connexion it will be borne in mind that as social integration proceeds administration will tend to become progressively more limited by general rules. It remains for international administrative law to be developed in the future. Meanwhile a constant regard for the general welfare and deference to the social imperative and public opinion will go far to supply the want of more specific guidance.

PROPOSITION XV.—In order that peace may be maintained administrative action is as necessary as insistence upon general rules in the society of states.

CHAPTER XVI

RIGHT AND MIGHT

SOME obscurity of thought as to the relation
between right and might is still widely prevalent.

Right and might are obviously very different
things. But there is no natural or necessary opposition between them.

Every one understands what might is. Most
people understand, for the immediate practical
purposes of their lives, what right is.

The ultimate object of all moral wisdom is to
elevate mankind at large to a state in which every
one, in pursuance of the guidance of his own conscience, will do what is right—will willingly concede
to others the same freedom of action that he desires
for himself—will do to others what he would wish
them to do to him. In this, the ideal condition of
society, right would prevail universally by virtue of
the goodwill of all. It would be adequately supported by the general moral sense. Might would
never be applied so as to contravene right. No
might would be necessary, therefore, for the active
support of right.

Up to the present time, however, a very large
proportion of mankind fall far short of this ideal
moral attitude. They cannot be trusted always to
respect right for its own sake. Accordingly, in

order that there may be a reasonable certainty that right shall prevail, it must be enforceable : the power of securing its observance by force if necessary must reside in those who are prepared to act in its support. The existence of the right, in the sense of moral (as distinguished from legal) right, is entirely independent of might ; but the enforceability of right is wholly dependent upon might. Right when opposed by might is in itself utterly powerless.

The use of phrases which imply that right is in itself a power is due partly to a tendency to the employment of metaphorical or elliptical language. It is commonly observed that a person or nation who assert a right often prevail against apparently overwhelming or preponderant forces arrayed in opposition to them. The facts of course are that, owing to the moral advancement already achieved by the race, people who believe they are fighting for right very commonly fight better—in other words, use more effective force—than those who are not animated by this motive ; and they also attract to their support other people or nations who are anxious to see right prevail.

Nothing, however, can be clearer than that might can be overcome only by greater might. When right is opposed by might it can prevail only if preponderating might is brought to bear in its support. Moral teaching may induce the mighty to refrain from exercising their might in contravention of right ; but nothing save greater force can ever have supremacy over force.

One would naturally have thought that the Great War would have rendered these propositions so obvious that their statement would be unnecessary. For when once the might of the Central Powers invaded Belgium nothing but the opposition of an equal or greater might could possibly have maintained the right of that country. Nevertheless, even during the continuance of the stupendous struggle, much was said about the necessity of establishing for the future the supremacy of right over force. And expressions such as these, however they may be understood by those who use them, are apt to prove the source of deplorable confusion in the minds of others.

The proper object of all men of goodwill is to ensure that right should be supported by as much might as is possible or necessary for its enforcement. Speaking generally of all mankind, whether considered as individuals or as associated in communities, it may be said that their immediate practical aim should be (1) to induce as many people as possible voluntarily to refrain from forcibly contravening the rights of others, and (2) to induce as many people as possible to be ready and willing to bring their might to bear against the might of any who may threaten or actually violate the rights of others.

' Violence and injustice shall be mastered by the sovereign alliance of force and right.' [1]

This is of cardinal importance as applied to our present subject.

There are, however, many earnest people who in varying terms propound the dangerous fallacy that the love of peace ought to preclude any provision for warlike measures for the sake of maintaining it. It

[1] M. Poincaré at Gonesse on 7th October 1915.

is therefore still necessary to insist upon the rationale of the sanction of force.

One must in this matter distinguish between the immediate object and the ultimate purpose.

The love of personal freedom and order does not exclude in municipal life the provision of a penalty for crime. The purpose of a sanction—or penalty—is not that it may itself be enforced but that the probability of its infliction in a certain contingency should prevent the occurrence of that contingency and the actual infliction of the penalty itself.

A League of Peace is necessary, because without it there would be wars. In order to prevent wars the means appropriate in that behalf must be adopted. The waging of war by an individual state can be prevented only by the probability that it would be rendered abortive by war on the part of others. War against law-breaking war is war for peace.

The greater the probability that wrongful war will be overcome by rightful war, the less will be the likelihood of wrongful war. When it is generally recognized as certain that wrongful war will be unsuccessful it will be very unlikely to occur.

In preceding chapters we have dealt with the development of moral forces. We have seen that, while there are solid grounds for believing in the increasing efficacy of these forces in preventing wars, for many years to come it will not be safe to rely on them alone.

We are now engaged upon a different phase of the subject. Right in itself being powerless against might, we have to consider the means of preventing wars by force. Accordingly, we must concentrate our attention for the time being on might. The problem is how to secure that a preponderance of might shall be on the side of those who wish to uphold the right.

PROPOSITION XVI.—Right is secure against the might of wrongdoers only if it is itself supported by the greater might of others.

CHAPTER XVII

THE GREAT POWERS

THE jural principles and the administrative machinery which would have been appropriate in a world divided with approximate equality between all its separate states are inapplicable to, and would be ineffective in, the world as it now actually exists. The facts must be accepted as they are found to be, and international arrangements must be conceived accordingly.

Looking backward we perceive that mankind considered in the aggregate have already made vast progress towards universal order and peace, and that this achievement has for the most part been due, so far as political arrangements are concerned, to the comprehension of the majority of the race within a comparatively few great states, rather than to the recognition by the several states of equal rights on the part of each against all the others under a common international system. The progress of the world has in fact been by the way of the building up of great political unions, rather than by that of the practical recognition of the equal rights of all states regardless of their size.

The potential quasi-sovereignty of the world is now inherent in the Great Powers. Its actuality is conditional only upon their collective willingness to exercise it. So far as they can act harmoniously peace can be maintained among the two thousand

millions of the inhabitants of the world. Without
their co-operation no other states can in any way
provide a stable foundation for a superstructure of
social order or guarantee the general security.
The power, the duty, and the burden of maintaining
these rest with the great states and, substantially,
with them only. The due formulation and expression of the opinions and advice of the lesser
states and their proportional influence in the
formation of international policy are, of course,
essential to the satisfactory working of the world
system. They can assist the Great Powers in
taking a right course, and if these Powers are
divided, they may effectively throw their own
weight upon the right side. But in the matter of
force—the ultimate sanction—their ability and
responsibility in reference to the maintenance of
order is collectively and severally so much less
than that of the Great Powers that there is a difference of kind as well as of degree between the
functions of these Powers and their own.

In this connexion certain moral considerations
are deserving of attention.

Where a duly constituted supreme authority
exists (as in the case of every civilized state) it is,
generally speaking, the duty of all the citizens
subject thereto, both individually and in association, to refrain from any acts which would constitute
an encroachment upon the monopoly of power
residing in the government. None but those who
act as ministers of the supreme authority ought
to arrogate to themselves the exercise of any powers
which properly pertain to that authority. This is so,
not only because the authority is normally adequate

for the preservation of order, but because the forcible intervention of unofficial individuals, though it might prove useful in particular instances, would in the long run tend to undermine the lawfully constituted authority and so to disturb the peace rather than to conserve it.

Where, on the other hand, although a society exists, no supreme authority has been developed, the case is essentially different. There, if disturbance of order is to be checked, or violent injury punished, individual members must assume the responsibility of taking the initiative. Intervention for the common welfare, though not authorized by any previous constitutional or conventional selection, so far from being treasonable or anarchical, is the only means of saving the society from confusion. Under such circumstances they who have the power to constrain their fellows—whether it be due to physical prowess, intellectual ability, or energy of character—are morally bound to exercise it for the common weal. They become responsible for taking the initiative. The possession of power to check violence and avoid chaos involves the moral obligation to exercise it effectively. In the case supposed, the society as such has no organized collective force : its power is distributed among its members. If therefore the exertion of force becomes necessary, it is from the members as such that it must proceed.

Now the society of states bears an obvious analogy to a society of individuals in which no supreme authority has been set up. Accordingly, the fact that the Powers can preserve the peace of the world if they choose to do so, casts upon them the moral responsibility to the world as a whole for taking the measures necessary to attain this object. Their ability in this behalf is virtually recognized by the very term, ' the Powers,' which has long been in general use. Their prerogative and duty to exercise this ability has been, as we have seen, tacitly admitted for centuries. In this behalf reason reinforces the propriety of the attitude which has been established by persistent practice.

It is, moreover, constantly to be borne in mind that a state is essentially an artificial entity, and is in itself of no real importance except in so far as it subserves the welfare and progress of the people who constitute its citizens. Individual beings alone are the ultimate object of all rational solicitude. Accordingly, so far as the Powers, by virtue of their ability to preserve the peace of the world outside their own borders, are charged with the moral duty of doing so, the duty is in the last resort to the peoples of the small states rather than to those states themselves.

At present we are considering how peace can be preserved forcibly. We must therefore think for the time being in terms of power, and be careful not to lose sight of the realities which dominate the situation.

If the Great Powers will refrain from fighting among themselves and act collectively to prevent strife outside their own borders the peace of the world can be secured.[1]

The practical problem is therefore narrowed to this—how can we prevent each and every of some eight or nine political entities from fighting any or

[1] In this connexion reference may usefully be made to the observations of Sir Eric Drummond on the Four-Power Pact in his speech at Queen's Hall on the 6th July 1933.

all of the rest ; and at the same time secure their collective action in preventing strife between any of the smaller states ?

The twofold aspect of this problem in itself suggests the key to its solution.   The negative object of any association will be furthered in proportion to the degree in which it is naturally incidental to the measures taken for the attainment of a positive object.   Agreeably to this general principle, the object of preventing the Powers from making war upon one another will be attained in proportion to the degree to which they can be induced to act together in taking the measures necessary for the welfare of the world as a whole.   A League of Peace, if it is to be successful, must have a positive as well as a negative aspect.   It must charge the Powers collectively with the active duty of taking the appropriate steps for the preservation of World-Peace.

The Great Powers have indeed long exercised from time to time a controlling authority over the smaller states.   Examples of this aspect of modern history have been given in preceding chapters. Regarding the world as a rudimentary social organism it may fairly be said that the process of differentiation of function has already resulted in the development of an organ of control.   In the development of a common will in the exercise of this organ lie the best hopes for the immediate future. The other conditions for the establishment of order are available.

PROPOSITION XVII.—The primary condition of the maintenance of peace is the co-operation of the Great Powers.

CHAPTER XVIII

THE WILL FOR PEACE

PEACE is the common interest of the entire world. In order that it may be preserved, appropriate administrative action must, from time to time, be taken on behalf of the society of states, and adequate forces must be available for the prevention or termination of hostilities. The practical problem in which every one is interested, whether consciously or not, is this—how is the world to make provision that such action shall be taken, and such forces shall be available, as may be necessary for the preservation of peace ?

It is of cardinal importance that the disposition to make whatever provisions may appear to be best calculated to prevent wars is now widespread and earnest. The tendencies in the direction of the peaceful settlement of international disputes which had been developing up to the month of August 1914, have been greatly accelerated by the impression made upon the minds of all civilized people by the events which have since occurred.

War, as it must henceforth be waged by great states, if waged at all, is now perceived to be a struggle in which the entire population and resources of the belligerents will be engaged with mutually disastrous and wholly incalculable results. Its horrible evils have been brought home even to the civilian inhabitants of the most advanced countries with appalling and decisive force.

Moreover, owing to the recent development of aviation and of chemical means of attack, the prospect of the employment in any great war of the future of methods of destruction far more widely effective than any which have hitherto been available has powerfully reinforced the lessons of personal experience. ' In the next war,' said Mr. Stanley Baldwin,[1] ' you will find that any town which is within reach of an aerodrome can be bombed within the first five minutes of war from the air, to an extent which was inconceivable in the last war, and the question will be, whose moral will be shattered quickest by that preliminary bombing ? I think it is well also for the man in the street to realize that there is no power on earth that can protect him from being bombed. Whatever people may tell him, the bomber will always get through. . . . Aerial war is still in its infancy, and its potentialities are incalculable and inconceivable.'

It is now indeed obvious to every one that hardly any object, except the preservation of civilization or of national existence, can be worth pursuing at the cost of such a war. Martial glory for its own sake no longer fascinates the imagination of mankind. Civilized people all over the world are bent upon having peace in their own time, and they would like to feel that provision had been made to secure it for their descendants too. They are accordingly prepared to adopt the measures which

---

[1] Speaking on the 10th November 1932 in the House of Commons.

may appear to them best calculated to afford this security.

The War has also had a vast effect in developing the organism and features of a world-society. It has quickened and intensified the process of social integration throughout by far the greater part of mankind. The fact that a dispute between Austria and Serbia led to a war, in which all the Powers as well as many minor states became involved, has most forcibly demonstrated the community of interest which now unites the different peoples of the earth. It has become manifest that the various races are in reality members of one body, and that all are concerned in the welfare and the sufferings of each. Moreover, by the solidarity of the Allies with regard to the objects which they so long pursued together, as well as by the suffering and sorrows which they bore in common, relations which are essentially social were developed to a high degree between representatives of most of the greatest states and nations. And it is especially to be remembered that the British Empire, within a few days of the outbreak of hostilities, declared war, which it continued to wage till the end, in order to uphold public right in the society of states. By this great example it prepared the way for the general acceptance of the principle of the several and collective responsibility of all states for the preservation of peace throughout the world.

In the result, there is now a strong tendency towards a general belief in the possibility of collective action with the object of preventing wars in the future.

Accordingly, the desire for peace which formerly

was felt in varying strength by an ever-increasing number of thoughtful people throughout the world is now hardening into a mandate of the general will of civilized mankind that, as far as practicable, wars shall be prevented.

' The combined impulses which work through political agencies can, in the absence of such agencies, produce others through which to work.' [1]   In any society of men where law does not prevail, there are generally to be found influential men ready to take the initiative in rallying the forces of order, and sufficient good sense on the part of others to support them effectively, in the suppression of violent wrongdoing.   In the wider society of states analogous conditions are being developed.

PROPOSITION XVIII.—In the world-society as a whole there is now a prevailing disposition towards organization for the maintenance of peace.

[1] Herbert Spencer's *Principles of Sociology*, vol. ii. p. 330.

CHAPTER XIX

DISARMAMENT AND SECURITY

COVENANTS to refrain from war and other moral and intellectual influences will do much to predispose peoples and governments in favour of the pacific settlement of all disputes and to obviate the development of dangerous hostilities. But in the international society, as in municipal communities, occasions will arise when nothing but the apprehension of the application of superior force will prevent the violent assertion of individual claims. Public right, if it is uniformly to prevail, must in the last resort rest upon the public might. Accordingly, there is a necessity for the existence of some power on which the separate states can respectively found a confident assurance that their rights will be recognized by all and in case of necessity adequately enforced.

The world-society must then make up its mind whether henceforth its members are each to rely upon its own strength or whether they are all to place their confidence in the collective force of the whole. If the decision is in favour of the latter course, it is clear that the states must be associated together as members of a league for peace. The essential conditions of such a league, if it is to be fully effective for its purpose, will now be considered. The amendments which are thus found to be necessary in the Covenant of the League of Nations will be dealt with specifically in the final chapter of this treatise.

It is obviously desirable that all the civilized peoples should be comprised in the league for peace. Its constitution and efficiency cannot be completely satisfactory until every Great Power is a party to its covenants. Meanwhile, however, the principles which would be applicable to a fully comprehensive league must be practically adjusted to the existing situation. But if the existing League of Nations acts as far as possible in the same way as a fully comprehensive league should act, it will probably be pursuing the course most likely to attract into its membership those states which now remain outside. In any case, in order to avoid embarrassing prolixity in what follows, it seems most convenient to speak of a league including all the states of the world. For the most part, what is so stated will be found applicable, *mutatis mutandis*, to the existing position of the League of Nations. Any qualifications which may be appropriate in this connexion will, it is conceived, readily present themselves to the mind of the reader.

The problems connected with disarmament and security are at once the most difficult and the most important which have to be solved before the organization of the international society for peace can be placed upon a satisfactory foundation. But the guiding principles which necessarily govern the appropriate treatment of these subjects are clearly ascertainable and susceptible of brief and simple statement. Indeed, in spite of the vast accumulation of literature by which they have been obscured, these principles will be found, upon careful consideration of the few essential factors involved, to be in reality almost self-evident.

We have already seen that, in order that peace may be established securely, it is necessary to create a standing probability that any belligerent operations not sanctioned by the League will be overcome by the exercise of a force sufficient for this purpose. Without this probability general security and permanent peace can never be completely established.

The function of force in this connexion is the same as it is in the individual state. The fact of the existence of the necessary force in the international society would render its actual exercise unnecessary except in occasional instances, as is already the case with the sanctions by which order is enforced in municipal societies. In every community alike, in proportion as the probability of the exercise of force in appropriate cases increases, the occasions for its actual exercise must diminish in frequency.

From the nature of the case there can be only one way in which the necessary sanction can be most effectually provided in the international world. The League must have at its disposal when necessary a collective force greater than any which is likely to be available to those who break the peace. In order that this may be so the Great Powers must covenant together that, on the summons of the Council of the League, they will respectively contribute an agreed quota to a common force, which collectively will be sufficiently strong to suppress any belligerent operations which may be conducted without the authority of the League.

It is sufficient in this connexion to speak only of the Great Powers for reasons indicated in Chapter XVII. Naturally, however, in any arrangements made with regard to security and disarmament, some of the other states would participate.

Such a covenant for mutual assistance in the maintenance of order is a condition precedent of disarmament on the part of individual Powers to the extent which is in itself necessary in order that general security may be established. Until each Power can rely upon the assistance in a proper case of the other Powers to an agreed extent, it will naturally rely primarily upon its own strength. And so long as this is the position—so long as each Power relies upon its own strength for use in case of need against others—armaments will be maintained by all the Powers which will necessarily constitute a standing menace to peace. Only when all armaments are avowedly and obviously maintained in the interests of general peace and security alone will the confidence of all rest upon a firm and reasonable basis.

At this stage of the argument it is of vital importance to bear in mind that, in order that a community or an individual should think it wise to make provision by insurance or otherwise against any particular danger, the cost of such provision must not be so great that the party concerned will prefer to leave the risk uncovered.

And if the great Powers were to continue to be free to increase their armaments at their own discretion, the burden of maintaining the quotas which would then be necessary in order to provide a sufficient collective force for the purpose of establishing the sanction required might well appear to some of the Powers an intolerable evil. On this hypothesis indeed the provision of the suggested sanction is apparently not a matter of practical politics. An imaginary illustration may render this proposition obvious. Let it be supposed that some Power or Powers were now in possession of armaments of the most modern types, equivalent in relative strength to those which were possessed by Germany and her allies in August 1914. In such circumstances the burden on all the other Great Powers of maintaining armaments sufficiently powerful to render it certain that belligerent operations on the part of the former Power or Powers would be overwhelmed immediately, or at least without grave difficulty and protracted warfare, would be a greater evil economically and otherwise than some at all events of the other Powers would be willing to endure.

It follows that the sanction necessary for security and peace can be provided only by means of two equally important and completely interdependent measures. Armaments must be made available by the Great Powers, in pursuance of their respective covenants in that behalf, sufficient collectively to overcome any belligerent operations on the part of law-breaking states. And there must also be disarmament by each Power down to the limit mutually agreed. Without the fulfilment of both these conditions concurrently, no Great Power can with safety either enter into the covenant proposed or disarm to the limit contemplated. In short, there can be no security without disarmament, and there will be no satisfactory disarmament without security.

The extent of the disarmament which is desirable, or, in other words, the standard by which the limitation of armaments should be fixed, is prescribed by the nature and circumstances of the case. Whenever the Great Powers should have agreed together to provide the proposed sanction for security and peace, it would be evident that they had respectively determined to rely for their own safety upon the existence of that sanction and not upon their own individual strength. There would accordingly be no good reason why any Power should wish to maintain armaments beyond those which it had agreed to supply to the common force, except to the extent necessary for such legitimate purposes of its own as the preservation of order in outlying territories bordering upon regions inhabited by races still uncivilized, the protection of particular routes, or internal police. The maintenance of any further armaments would indeed be inconsistent with the basic principle of the new provision for security. It would also be an obvious menace to the other contracting parties inasmuch as such forces might be used in contravention of the provisions of the covenanted scheme. It would therefore tend to the increase of the burden of the necessary armaments of other Powers beyond that which was required by the common weal. The possession of excessive forces by any Power must, indeed, in itself render the successful action of the League in possible contingencies uncertain or even impracticable

Whether the very small states should undertake

to co-operate actively in military measures decreed by the Council to be necessary may be doubted. All states should, however, be under an obligation to facilitate the operations undertaken in pursuance of the general will and for the common benefit. Accordingly it should be provided that, when the Powers are engaged upon military operations for the purpose of restoring peace, they should be free to carry out any measures deemed to be necessary within the territories of the other states. Only so could the Powers command the proper facilities for putting the maximum stress upon a recalcitrant state or states, whether by investment, blockade, or otherwise. It might even be desirable to extend this freedom of operation to cases where, without actually making war, the League should adopt measures of constraint against a particular state.[1]

The vast benefits which the League would secure for small states would not be purchased too dearly by this obligation on their part to passive assistance in the operations necessary for the fulfilment of the functions of the organization. It is, moreover, evidently in accordance with justice that, where the Powers would be striving for the general security, their operations should not be hampered by any single state. From a practical standpoint, moreover, it is clear that the freedom of the League to operate anywhere and everywhere would tend greatly to accelerate the success of their arms and to keep the sufferings and inconveniences incident to hostilities within the narrowest limits possible.

[1] Article 16, clause 3, of the Covenant of the League of Nations goes far in this direction.

The reciprocal undertakings between the parties to the League to concur in measures for the preservation of peace of course completely differentiates the League from an alliance the proximate object of which is only the interest of the contracting parties themselves.

It is clear that the quotas of armed forces required to be maintained by the Great Powers respectively at the disposition of the League would be diminished as peace and order throughout the world became increasingly secure. And this diminution would, as it were automatically, be accelerated by its own operation. Indeed, in a world in which all states were members of the League it might—theoretically at all events— reach the vanishing point. Inasmuch as the quotas would be necessary only for the purpose of overcoming any forces of law-breakers, when these latter forces no longer existed, the *raison d'être* of the quotas themselves would cease. Armed forces could then be limited to those which in their nature were merely the police of the states maintaining them.

The essential connexion between disarmament and security may be illustrated by the development of the reign of law and the accompanying decline of self-redress in the various states throughout the world. To speak of England only, it is clear that the King's Peace was never satisfactorily assured until, after the contentions of centuries, the fortification of castles by individual subjects was successfully restrained and the power of the central government became sufficient to overcome easily any forces available for its resistance.

It may be suggested that the scheme leaves open the possibility that some one or more of the Powers might refuse to supply its agreed quota when duly called upon to do so. But if the scheme promises a greater probability of stability than that which is enjoyed in the circumstances of the existing international position, and greater also than that which would be provided by any other scheme which is likely to be adopted, its defects, however important, cannot warrant its non-acceptance.

Some will perhaps suggest that the Great Powers might act oppressively with regard to the other states. The provisions, however, which would naturally be made for the necessity of a considerable majority of votes before the collective force could be employed, would go far to obviate any real risk in this direction.[1]   Moreover, the admission of such an objection would be fatal to world-order in any practicable form.

It may also, of course, be objected that the covenanting Powers might quarrel among themselves. If, however, this occurred, the situation would be analogous to that produced by civil war within an individual state ; and against such a contingency it is not theoretically possible to provide. But as soon as the suggested disarmament had been effected—as soon as every Power had reduced its forces to the standard agreed upon for its quota available for the purposes of the League and its own police—the danger of a breakdown of the machinery of the League, or of forcible resistance to its decisions, would necessarily rapidly diminish. No state which had once thrown in its

[1] These provisions are discussed in the following chapters.

lot whole-heartedly with the League and had deliberately determined to look to it, and to it alone, for the maintenance of its rights and its protection from forcible injury, would be likely to commit so wanton and dangerous an outrage as the waging of war against its colleagues. And the indisposition to adopt such a course would naturally increase as the whole world grew accustomed to the normal operation of the beneficent agencies of peace.

In any case it is of cardinal importance in the consideration of this subject to recognize that the suggested scheme provides the *only complete solution* of a difficulty which every one can see has to be faced. No Great Power will be justified in relying for its security upon the League until provisions substantially similar in their nature and extent have in fact been made. If, therefore, it is not practicable to bring it into operation in the near future, it may still be useful as the ideal towards which we should constantly endeavour to approach.

In this connexion it is important to bear in mind that the view which is set forth above is, in substance, the conclusion which has been reached by many—perhaps one should say by most—of the leading statesmen and writers who have devoted special attention to the matter. A few representative expressions of opinion may usefully be cited by way of illustration.

President Woodrow Wilson, addressing the Senate of the United States of America on the 22nd January 1917, said : ' In every discussion of the peace that must end this war, it is taken for granted that that peace must be followed by some definite concert of power which will make it virtually impossible that any such catastrophe should ever overwhelm us again. . . . Mere agreements may not make peace secure. It will be absolutely necessary that a force be created as a guarantor of the permanency of the settlement so much greater than the force of any nation now engaged or any alliance hitherto formed or projected that no nation, no probable combination of nations, could face or withstand it. If the peace presently to be made is to endure, it must be a peace made secure by the organized major force of mankind. . . . There must be, not a balance of power, but a community of power. . . . Right must be based upon the common strength, not upon the individual strength, of the nations upon whose concert peace will depend. . . . There can be no sense of safety and equality among the nations if great preponderating armaments are henceforth to continue here and there to be built up and maintained. . . . I am proposing that all nations henceforth avoid entangling alliances which would draw them into competitions of power. . . . There is no entangling alliance in a concert of power. When all unite to act in the same sense and with the same purpose, all act in the common interest and are free to live their own lives under a common protection.' And in the course of a speech made in the United States, while the Peace Conference was in session, the President said : ' The arrangements of the present peace cannot stand a generation unless they are guaranteed by the united forces of the civilized world.'

Matthias Erzberger wrote : ' That the League of Nations must have means of enforcing its will, in order that it may proceed against every infringer of the peace, is self-evident.' ' The second essential to the foundations of the League of Nations, after compulsory arbitration, is disarmament.' ' Confidence in a peace of international justice must be founded on the abolition of the menace underlying the general system of armaments.   Disarmament—and disarmament by land and water both—is thus an essential element of the stipulations which must be fulfilled in order that the nations may bind themselves together in a League of Nations.' [1]

Lord Cecil of Chelwood says : ' I thought and still think an international agreement to limit armaments is essential if an enduring peace is to be attained. . . . I recognize that force may still be an unavoidable element in international as it is in national life.   But it must be the force of the whole community directed against the law-breaker, and not legalized international brigandage.   National armaments must be regarded as the contribution of each state to the force required to preserve the peace of the world rather than a precaution necessary for the national safety.   They must be looked upon as a burden and not a privilege, and if their limitation be approached in that spirit the problem should not be insoluble.' [2]   Again Lord Cecil says : ' That a common army can be maintained by the states of Europe is not at present within the range of practical politics.   But it is

---

[1] *The League of Nations*, by M. Erzberger, translated by B. Miall, and published in England in 1919 ; at pp. 109, 188, 204.

[2] *The Way of Peace*, pp. 9, 10.

conceivable that the armies of all the states should
be maintained for one common purpose, namely,
the preservation of peace ; and many of us believe
that it is upon that footing that the armies not only
of Europe but of England and America should be
considered. Had that view been the governing
view during the recent [1] negotiations at Geneva,
agreement would have been not only possible but
easy. What, then, of the future ? If we are to
listen to the teaching of history we must perceive
that the line of progress is the line of international
co-operation. That must be fostered by all means
in our power.' [2] And again : ' Personally, I am
convinced that you will never get a complete and
effective disarmament treaty unless the question
of security is tackled. Continental countries, that
is to say, will never lay down their arms or even
seriously diminish their armed forces unless they
are satisfied that if they do so they will be protected
from sudden and treacherous attacks from their
neighbours.[3]

Partial disarmament, such as hitherto has
occupied the attention of international conferences
(that is to say, the limitation of armaments apart
from the execution of a general covenant for the
contribution by each Power of specified contingents
towards a common military and naval force), may
of course relieve economic pressure, and so far as
it goes, promote a general disposition towards
peace and the confidence of mankind in its maintenance. But its effects must differ in kind as well
as in degree from the disarmament which is out-

---

[1] *The Way of Peace* was published in 1928.
[2] *The Way of Peace*, p. 122.   [3] *Ibid.* p. 175.

lined above as an essential feature in a scheme for general security. Considered apart from such a scheme, armaments retain the character and function of a means of self-protection and redress, on the part of the Power which possesses them, as against the forces of other Powers. There is, in this case, no reliable standard by which the extent to which disarmament ought to be carried can be ascertained. It can be agreed, if at all, only as the result of divers and conflicting motives in the form of a compromise which bears, in itself, no inherent likelihood of proving either satisfactory or permanent.

The comparative failure of disarmament conferences up to the present time is therefore no matter for surprise. It is naturally difficult to arrive at agreement upon practical measures so long as no rational principle to which they can be referred has been accepted. It is *a priori* an obvious truth, which lengthened discussion should have rendered generally apparent, that disarmament without security and security without disarmament cannot possibly be achieved satisfactorily.

Is there then any good reason why the Great Powers should not concur in the arrangements which are necessary in order to achieve the objects which all apparently desire ?

By the Pact of Locarno certain Powers have undertaken to go to war in the event of a notification by the Council of the League of Nations that it has found that a violation of one or other of certain articles of this treaty or of the treaty of Versailles has been committed by one of the other parties to the Pact, or in some circumstances without any such finding, although the former Powers would not, apart from this Pact, be directly and immediately concerned in the matter.

Moreover, speaking in Geneva on the 3rd February 1933, on behalf of the British Government, Mr. Eden was reported to have said that ' the British Government, in a spirit of realism, had abandoned the ambitious ideal of a universal effort towards mutual assistance, and sought rather to encourage a natural growth of the system of security in accordance with local and immediate necessities. In signing the Locarno Treaty they had sought to set an example which they hoped might be followed. That hope had been endorsed by the League Assembly itself. It had not yet been realized, but if groups of nations could devise similar means for meeting those regional perils which immediately beset them, these might, in themselves, prove to be a valuable contribution to the general sense of confidence and goodwill ' (*The Times*, 4th February 1933).

It seems, however, extremely improbable that any number of ' regional pacts ' would ever establish the general security. It is indeed hardly too much to say that it is self-evident that they could not have this result. Nor would they necessarily tend to encourage general disarmament to any satisfactory extent.

On the other hand, the realization of ' the ambitious ideal of a universal effort towards mutual assistance ' would have the supreme merit of being the only way in which general security could be obtained. And by it alone can rational disarmament ever be rendered practicable. Its benefits, too, would be acquired at the least possible cost. For the guarantee of mutual assistance would, as has been pointed out above, naturally involve only a limited liability—the undertaking to provide specified forces only—and so avoid the graver danger involved in the covenants of the guaranteeing Powers in treaties like that of Locarno. There is also another consideration which, from the point of view of practical politics, is probably more important than any of the foregoing. A scheme for general security is calculated to appeal to the altruism of the modern mind with incomparably greater power than a system conceived with a view merely to ' local and immediate necessities,' or, in other words, the primarily self-regarding motives of any particular group of states.

AIR FORCES

In the case of air forces it may well be found better to adopt a scheme of international regulation rather than that of mutual covenants for the contribution by the Powers of agreed quotas to a common force.

Aerial traffic occupies a position peculiar to itself. Transit on land, whether by railway, road, or otherwise, is subject to the control of the particular state through whose territory it is for the time being taking place. Transit by water, if upon the high seas, is subject to no territorial jurisdiction, because it does not pass through or over any area appropriated to the control or ownership of any particular Power ; while, so far as it passes over territorial waters, it is subject, like transit on land, to the jurisdiction of the Power which controls them.

Transit through the air differs from each of the foregoing. Although the air is *res communis*, aircraft, while over land, are subject to the possibility of some control on the part of the territorial Power, and, by reason of the contingency of descent and other considerations, this Power is for the time being not wholly uninterested in their passage. Moreover, a widely prevalent rule of civil law prescribes that *cujus est solum ejus est usque ad coelum*. On the other hand, as aeroplanes and airships pass rapidly, and often at considerable height, over territorial boundaries, the actual exercise of effective control by particular states over whose territory they pass is largely impracticable or inconvenient.

Accordingly there is a strong *primâ facie* case for the exercise by the states of the world collectively of jurisdiction and control over aircraft. This is powerfully reinforced by two considerations in connexion with the maintenance of peace. The airship or aeroplane constructed for the purpose of commercial transport can readily be adapted for the uses of war. At the same time these uses are of such a nature that the provision of adequate means of defence against their sudden and unforeseen application is extremely difficult, if not impracticable.

Accordingly it seems manifest that it would be in the general interest that the Council of the League of Nations should have an effective control over all air vessels, which would enable it in case of necessity to assume the direction of their movements and custody. By the exercise of this power in proper cases it would as far as practicable prevent the wrongful use of air forces against any particular state and at the same time be provided with the most powerful means of giving effect to its own decisions for the common good.

Such an international control of aerial navigation would not be without analogies in municipal law. The ownership of firearms, the traffic in poisons, and the transport of dangerous substances are commonly regulated by various restrictive rules.

The precise form of the necessary arrangements in respect of aircraft will no doubt be the subject of much discussion. It is, however, clear that it by no means passes the wit of man to devise a satisfactory scheme for their control. The normal freedom in their use of the corporations or individuals invested with their beneficial ownership, can, indeed, easily be reconciled with an overriding right on the part of the Council of the League to dispose of them in case of need.

PROPOSITION XIX.—Limitation of armaments and mutual covenants for security on the part of the Great Powers are necessary and concurrent conditions of the permanent maintenance of peace.

CHAPTER XX

THE ADMINISTRATIVE AUTHORITY

WE have seen that in the last resort the only sanction effective to restrain each and every state from breaking the peace would be the recognized ability of the law-abiding states to mobilize a preponderating force. The provision of this sanction necessitates not only the availability of armed forces for the service of the common cause but the existence of an authority empowered to determine when and how these resources shall be brought into activity. There could not otherwise be any reasonable certainty that appropriate action would be taken when circumstances rendered it necessary. If it were left to be determined by reference to any general rule, such as, for instance, that the forces of the League should be used, and used only, against an ' aggressor ' or an ' invader ' defined in a particular way, the issue might well be left open to doubt at the critical time. Rules would, of course, be available for the guidance of those who constituted the authority, but they alone should be the judges of the applicability of a particular rule in any actual circumstances. This is a necessary condition of the existence of a standing probability of effective action against transgressors.

Quite apart, however, from the necessity for the

existence of an administrative authority in order
that the ultimate sanction of force may be effectively
operative, the constitution of such an authority is
an indispensable feature of an effective organization
for the maintenance of peace for the reasons stated
in Chapter XV. An authority competent in the
last resort to determine any dispute between states
which cannot otherwise be adjusted peaceably is
indeed the keystone of the arch of international
justice and order, without which the edifice can
never be complete.

Covenants in restraint of war and other agencies
for the preservation of peace will never be completely
effective unless all that formerly could usefully and,
in a sense, properly be attained by war is rendered
attainable in the future by other means. It will
never be enough for a League to agree and declare
that war shall not be permitted. If it is to succeed
in regard to this negative object, it must itself be
endowed with a positive function. While it pre
vents any state or nation from asserting a claim by
war, it must see that a state against which a claim
is made does not withhold what justice and expediency require that it should concede.

Where a claim is of a legal character an adequate
Court is already available for its decision. Where
it is of a nature outside the scope of jurisprudence,
methods of conciliation, mediation, or arbitration are
also available. But wherever, owing to the failure
of the parties to concur in any course for the settlement of their differences, or for any other reason,
no decision is reached and the administrative
authority is accordingly confronted with a controversy which cannot otherwise be determined, it

must be empowered to pronounce its own award and so preserve the peace in the only way consonant with justice and the general good.

It has been pointed out in Chapter II that the continual changes in the relative strength and territorial needs of states due to the increase or decline in numbers and virility of the various nations, as well as certain other causes, have hitherto, from time to time, given rise to a kind of natural necessity for the alteration of frontiers, which has generally been accomplished only at the cost of war. The same kind of necessity will still occur in the future, although it may be with less frequency or urgency than formerly owing to that decline of anti-social nationalism which will not improbably gradually take place concurrently with the development of the various agencies for peace and general goodwill. Moreover, demands may be made by governments on behalf of their nationals for means of access to the seas or to the sources of the supplies of raw materials alleged to be necessary for their economic development or prosperity, or for particular facilities for transport and transit, or for permission for their surplus populations to colonize unpopulated or thinly-peopled regions within the territorial boundaries of other states, as well as for the revision of particular treaties on other grounds. Even restrictions upon international trade may be brought into serious controversy. Whatever, indeed, the demands made by one state against another, they will call for determination, whether it takes the form of concession or rejection or some intermediate award.

The necessity for appropriate intervention from

time to time in the interests of minority populations has already been generally recognized, and
provision has been made for according it in several
international treaties.

Even before the League of Nations was formed
the objection was urged that its existence would lead
to a certain stability of political relations which
would be inconsistent with the need for development which would from time to time be experi-
enced by the states which were comprised within
it.   In dealing with this difficulty Herr Erzberger
said : ' What must be excluded from the future
international life of the nations are acts of violence.
It is not in the least at variance with this that a
state should extend its frontiers by a treaty in
accordance with the express wishes of the inhabitants of the districts concerned. The question
of territorial acquisitions, even peacefully carried
out, will, however, in future gradually lose its
importance for the nations, in proportion as the
increasing permeation of the whole of international
life by the ideal of justice does away with the
motive for territorial aggrandizement. Nations
have striven for territorial aggrandizement chiefly
because of the necessity of safe-guarding their
frontiers, or because of their need of raw materials.
If wars are to be avoided in future, the safe-guarding
of frontiers—think of aircraft and long-range guns
—will no longer be of much importance, and the
same is true of the system of buffer states ; while
the freedom of trade and commerce, and the
thorough recognition of the equal claim of all
nations upon the raw materials of the world, will
deprive the territorial question, considered in

connexion with the question of raw materials, of much of its consequence as a disturber of the peace. But the possibility of territorial development as such will exist even under the League of Nations. The League of Nations will not mean political atrophy. In the foreground of its existence is the idea that problems can no longer be successfully solved by force of arms, but by peaceful agreements, or by appeal to the court of arbitration.' [1]

At the same time any novelty in this proposal is more apparent than real. The Congresses of European Powers which have met from time to time for centuries, and the Concert of Europe since 1815, as well as the conferences which prepared the various treaties of peace at the conclusion of the Great War, have performed work which, although only occasional in character, as well as often inadequate or otherwise defective, was essentially similar both in respect of its objects and its methods to that which would be entrusted to the Authority here proposed. And from every point of view a permanent Authority would appear more likely to be satisfactory than one appointed *ad hoc*.

Moreover, the conception of such an organization has been to a large extent suggested by celebrated thinkers who, from time to time, have applied their minds to the subject of the prevention of war.

In the *De Jure Belli et Pacis* of Hugo Grotius there is one passage of vital interest and importance in this connexion. Treating of compromise or arbitration as one of the ways in which controversies may be prevented from breaking out into wars,

[1] *The League of Nations*, translated by B. Miall, pp. 302–3.

13

and after observing that ' especially are Christian kings and states bound to try this way of avoiding war,' he says : ' Both for this reason and for others, it would be useful, and indeed it is almost necessary, that certain Congresses of Christian Powers should be held, in which the controversies which arise among some of them may be decided by others who are not interested ; and in which measures may be taken to compel the parties to accept peace on equitable terms.' [1]

This, in the opinion of the present writer, is the golden sentence of the illustrious jurist. It contains in itself the germ and essential characteristics of the only scheme which bears any real promise of peace to mankind in general. One is tempted to wonder why Grotius himself did not accord to this suggestion a greater prominence than it in fact has in the system which he elaborated with so much patience and zeal.

The scheme which was given to the world in 1713 by the Abbé de Saint-Pierre was supposed to have been expanded from a plan prepared by the Duc de Sully and attributed by him to Henry IV of France. In Wheaton's *History of the Law of Nations* [2] this scheme [3] is thus summarized : ' The first article of the *projet* proposed to establish a perpetual alliance between the members of the European league, or Christian republic, for their mutual security against both foreign and civil war, and for the mutual guarantee of their respective possessions, and of the treaties of peace concluded at Utrecht. The 2nd article proposed that each

---

[1] Whewell's translation, bk. ii. cap. xxiii. sect. viii. 3, 4.
[2] Pp. 261-3.   [3] As developed in 1729.

ally should contribute to the common expenses of the grand alliance a monthly contribution to be regulated by the general assembly of their plenipotentiaries. The 3rd article provided that the allies should renounce the right of making war against each other, and accept the mediation and arbitration of the general assembly of the league for the termination of their mutual differences, three-fourths of the votes being necessary for a definitive judgment. The principal sovereigns and states who were to compose the league,' to the number of nineteen, were arranged in a certain order of precedence. 'Each of these nineteen powers was to have a single vote in the European diet, and the smaller republics and princes to be associated in the league, with the right of giving a single collective vote. . . . The 4th article stipulated that if any one of the allied Powers should refuse to carry into effect the judgments and regulations of the grand alliance, or negotiate treaties in contravention thereof, or prepare to wage war, the alliance should arm and' act offensively against the offending Power, until it was reduced to obedience. The 5th article declared that the general assembly of plenipotentiaries of the alliance should have power to enact by a plurality of votes all laws necessary to carry into effect the objects of the alliance ; but no alteration in the fundamental articles was to be made without the unanimous consent of the allies.'

This citation is sufficient to show that St. Pierre, like Grotius, had a firm hold upon the root of the matter ; and it is unnecessary to refer in this place to the criticisms, many of them of obvious validity, which have been freely passed upon the details of his scheme by Leibniz, Voltaire, Rousseau, and others.

A careful study of the writings of Kant, so far as they bear upon the present subject, makes it clear that the views of this philosopher as to the best means of maintaining peace underwent some fluctuation. His final opinion, however, appears to be expressed in the *Metaphysics of Jurisprudence*, published in 1797, as follows : [1] ' The establishment of perpetual peace, which ought to be considered as the ultimate object of every system of public law, may perhaps be considered as impracticable, inasmuch as the too great extension of . . . a federal union might render impossible that supervision over its several members, and that protection to each member which is essential to its ends. But the establishment of those principles which tend to further this object, by forming such alliances between different states as may gradually lead to its accomplishment, is by no means an impracticable idea, since it is grounded upon the rights and the duties of men and of states. Such a general association of states, having for its object the preservation of peace, might be termed the permanent congress of nations. Such was the diplomatic conference formed at The Hague during the first part of the eighteenth century, with a similar view, consisting of the ministers of the greater part of the European Courts and even of the smallest republics. In this manner all Europe was constituted into one federal state, of which the several members submitted their differences to the decision of this conference as their sovereign arbiter.

[1] See Wheaton's *History of the Law of Nations*, p. 753.

. . . What we mean to propose is a general congress of nations, of which both the meeting and the duration are to depend entirely on the sovereign wills of the several members of the league, and not an indissoluble union like that which exists between the several states of North America founded on a municipal constitution. Such a congress and such a league are the only means of realizing the idea of a true public law according to which the differences between nations would be determined by civil proceedings as those between individuals are determined by civil judicature, instead of resorting to war, a means of redress worthy only of barbarians.'

It thus appears that Grotius, St. Pierre, and Kant—the noble-minded jurist, the enthusiastic visionary, and the profound philosopher—all alike grasped the essential truth that *wars can be prevented only by the administrative action of the representatives of separate states acting collectively after deliberation in a common council.*

The practical conclusion then appears to be that, in order to secure the permanent maintenance of peace, there must be an administrative authority empowered to take cognizance of any interstatal relations or disputes by which war may be threatened in any part of the world—an authority which shall undertake in the last resort the function of forming and enforcing the decisions which may appear to it to be just and necessary. The constitution of this authority is, however, in reality the one great difficulty, both theoretically and practically, in the way of the establishment of permanent peace. It can, indeed, be accomplished only if the Great

Powers become willing to divest themselves of the most salient attribute of separate external sovereignty which they still possess.

The potential sovereignty of the whole world lies, as we have seen, with the Great Powers acting collectively; and a central administrative authority, if it is to be stable and efficient, must substantially and practically be mainly controlled by them. If there were vested in a majority, of which they or most of them did not necessarily form part, the right to issue orders which could be carried into effect only by the forces of these Powers, it is certain that a strain would be placed upon the machinery of peace which it could not support, and that confusion and impotence would ensue. On the other hand, a sufficient safeguard against unnecessary or unjustifiable interference by the administrative authority could be provided by the requirement, except in the case of measures for the suppression or prevention of actual or threatened war, that the decrees of the Council controlled by the Great Powers should be effective only if ratified by a majority of all the states belonging to the League.

An administrative jurisdiction will be amply justified by its necessity in order that the supreme object of the prevention of war may be attained. But it is evident also that small states will directly benefit by a system which secures to them the collective consideration of the League, acting in the general interest, in lieu of a precarious integrity, accompanied by the risk of arbitrary and cruel action on the part of individual Powers.

It must never be forgotten that the necessity for

the existence of such a League as we are considering arises from the admitted and obvious insufficiency of purely moral influences for the maintenance of peace ; and that the existence of the League as a restraining power involves *pro tanto* the limitation of the independence of all states respectively. ' Idcirco omnes servire sumus ut liberi esse possumus.'

The League can fulfil its supreme function of maintaining order only by intervention in the affairs of disputant states. In order that its intervention may be supported, not only by the physical power at its command, but by the moral approval of mankind—in other words, in order that its intervention may be reasonable and in the general interest—it must of necessity assume jurisdiction over all matters which involve the risk of international disorder.

PROPOSITION XX.—An Authority supported by the co-operation of the Powers and charged with the function of taking the administrative and executive measures necessary from time to time to prevent war is an essential feature in an efficient organization for the permanent maintenance of world-order.

CHAPTER XXI

THE LEAGUE OF NATIONS

WE have now reviewed the features which are theoretically essential in an effective league for peace. The way is therefore prepared for a critical examination of the existing League of Nations with the object of ascertaining the amendments in its constitution which are necessary in order that its deficiencies may be made good.

The League as at present constituted falls short of an efficient organization for the maintenance of peace in three respects :—1. It does not provide an authority empowered to determine every dispute between states which cannot be settled by other agencies even although the peace may be endangered by its continuance. 2. It does not provide for general security. 3. It does not provide for the satisfactory limitation of armaments.

Nevertheless, the Covenant of the League goes far in the direction of each of these *desiderata*.

Powers of the Council

The functions assigned to the Council by the Covenant are in effect a recognition by the signatories of the necessity of such an administrative authority as was discussed in the last chapter.

The powers, however, which are conferred upon this body are insufficient to enable it to deal effectively with the most important of the matters which are expressly brought within its constitutional cognizance. The Council, it is declared, may deal with any matter affecting the peace of the world. But it has not, even theoretically, the right to determine decisively disputes of the kinds which are specially likely to lead to wars. Nor is it provided, even in cases of the greatest emergency, with any means of obtaining the support which may be necessary for the efficacy of the resolutions at which it arrives. It has accordingly no power of affording general security or of rendering practicable such a limitation of armaments as is a necessary condition of the establishment of permanent peace.

Naturally, experience has shown that the inadequacy of the powers possessed by the Council involves grave danger to the continuance of the beneficent authority which it was evidently intended by the framers of the Covenant that it should freely exercise.

The ambiguous and unsatisfactory nature of the present position appears on a perusal of the clauses of the Covenant which deal particularly with the functions and proceedings of the Council.

' Article 4 (4). The Council may deal at its meetings with any matter within the sphere of action of the League or affecting the peace of the world.'

' Article 10. The members of the League undertake to respect and preserve as against external aggression the territorial integrity and existing

political independence of all members of the
League. In case of any such aggression or in case
of any threat or danger of such aggression the
Council shall advise upon the means by which this
obligation shall be fulfilled.'

'Article 11. 1. Any war or threat of war,
whether immediately affecting any of the Members of
the League or not, is hereby declared a matter of
concern to the whole League, and the League shall
take any action that may be deemed wise and
effectual to safeguard the peace of nations. In case
any such emergency should arise the Secretary-
General shall on the request of any Member of the
League forthwith summon a meeting of the Council.
2. It is also declared to be the friendly right of
each Member of the League to bring to the attention
of the Assembly or of the Council any circumstance
whatever affecting international relations which
threatens to disturb international peace or the
good understanding between nations upon which
peace depends.'

'Article 16. 1. Should any Member of the
League resort to war in disregard of its covenants
under Article 12, 13, or 15, it shall *ipso facto* be
deemed to have committed an act of war against
all other Members of the League. . . .

.   .   .   .

'2. It shall be the duty of the Council in such
case to recommend to the several Governments
concerned what effective military, naval, or air force
the Members of the League shall severally contribute to the armed forces to be used to protect the
covenants of the League.'

.   .   .   .

The Covenant thus clearly contemplates the use of a Collective Force contributed by the Members of the League for the purpose of overcoming lawless hostilities and maintaining the general peace. But it falls short of laying expressly upon any state the obligation to contribute a quota to that Force. The Council is to advise or recommend what it thinks necessary in this behalf; but there its authority ends. Nor is any provision made for the command of such forces as might voluntarily be placed at its disposal. And even this clause 2 of Article 16 is omitted from the new article which would be substituted for Article 16 if the necessary ratifications should be received.

The other provisions of Article 16 for the application of economic pressure, important as no doubt they are, obviously fall far short of the requirements of effective action for the maintenance of peace.

' Article 15. 1. If there should arise between Members of the League any dispute likely to lead to a rupture, which is not submitted to arbitration or judicial settlement in accordance with Article 13, the Members of the League agree that they will submit the matter to the Council. . . .

.   .   .   .

' 6. If a report of the Council is unanimously agreed to by the members thereof other than the Representatives of one or more of the parties to the dispute, the Members of the League agree that they will not go to war with any party to the dispute which complies with the recommendations of the report.'

.   .   .   .

It is unnecessary to set out any other of the clauses of this Article. It appears from those which have been cited that, in the circumstances most favourable to the authority of the Council, no effective means of enforcing its decision are provided. Clause 6 indeed appears to be in the nature of an anti-climax, and so obviously inadequate that it is difficult to imagine that any one could have supposed it to be otherwise.

" Article 19. The Assembly may from time to time advise the reconsideration by Members of the League of treaties which have become inapplicable and the consideration of international conditions whose continuance might endanger the peace of the world.'

Here again the inadequacy of the Covenant must, one would suppose, always have been evident.

It has been shown above that many, if not most, of the disputes which have caused wars in the past, could not have been satisfactorily settled by a court of justice bound to apply legal rules in its decisions, or even by arbitration as ordinarily understood. Such disputes have frequently involved a claim on the part of one state for the alteration of the conditions or relations subsisting between itself and another state. And the claim accordingly has not been based upon justice in the sense of conformity to some known rule of civil or international law, but upon considerations of necessity, or expediency, or of justice in the sense of conformity to an ideal ethical standard. Disputes arising from such claims will still cause the principal international difficulties of the future. The many questions indeed which are being agitated in connexion with the suggested revision of the treaties by which the Great War was terminated are in themselves salient instances of claims of such a nature. For the settlement of these matters the Covenant of the League affords no satisfactory or effective means. Yet is it not sufficiently clear that the only body qualified to determine such questions in the best way practicable is the League of Nations acting through its Council and Assembly ?

SECURITY AND DISARMAMENT

We have considered in previous chapters the essential elements of the sanction which is necessary in the last resort for the maintenance of peace. This sanction the League fails to provide.

There are at present no armed forces upon which the League can rely in order to maintain the Covenant inviolate. Its impotence in this respect has been strikingly demonstrated to the world at large, and its credit has accordingly been gravely impaired. In order that it should recover the prestige which it once enjoyed, it is apparent that its arm must be strengthened. Growth is now essential to its continued vigour.

It cannot reasonably be expected that states will abandon their means of self-protection and self-redress until a better method of upholding public right has become available. Until, therefore, in some way or other the League has been enabled to fulfil effectively the duties with which it is charged, every Great Power will naturally rely upon its own armaments for its own security, and the sanction necessary for the preservation of the general peace cannot exist. The whole course of the discussions which have taken place on the question of disarmament should have dispelled any illusions in regard to this matter. Their comparative futility has, indeed, been predestined by the very nature of the case. As soon, however, as an authority should be constituted to which every state could appeal, not only for the recognition of its rights, but for their enforcement, the problem of disarmament would at once admit of a rational solution.

Article 8 of the Covenant envisages disarmament ; but it deals with the subject by way of an executory agreement, which is not likely ever to be substantially implemented except *pari passu* with the execution of a mutual covenant for general security.

The necessary first step in this direction will, however, have been taken if the Great Powers should agree as to the limits of the forces which it is necessary for them respectively to provide for the common safety and for their own internal police and other analogous purposes. The Covenant for mutual assistance could then, without undue risk to any party, be entered into by all, with the proviso that its operation was to be postponed until the armaments of each had been brought into conformity with the limits so agreed. The way would thus be cleared for the actual diminution of armaments, which could then proceed, under the supervision of the Council of the League, by such stages as would, so far as practicable, maintain from time to time the subsisting relative strength of the armaments of the various Powers respectively, until the reduction of all had been completed in conformity with the general covenant.

And is it not obvious that this course is the only way of giving practical effect to the intention indicated in the Covenant itself ? For it is stated by the first clause of Article 8 that : ' The Members of the League recognize that the maintenance of peace requires the reduction of national armaments to the lowest point consistent with national safety and the enforcement by common action of international obligations.'

THE ESSENTIAL AGREEMENT

The provision of the force necessary for general security has been considered in Chapter XIX. Applying what has been there said to the League, amendments in the Covenant to the following effect are indicated as appropriate :

Each of the Great Powers covenants with the others that upon the request of the Council it will forthwith place armed forces not exceeding the specified limits at the disposition of the Council for the purpose of giving effect to any decision of the Council duly formed and promulgated in conformity with the provisions of the amended Covenant of the League.

Should any state resort to war otherwise than in pursuance of the request of the

Council or forcibly oppose a decision of the Council, it shall be the duty of the Council to call upon the Governments of the Great Powers for such military, naval, or air forces[1] within the specified limits as the Council shall think necessary, and to employ these forces in such ways and subject to such command or direction as it shall think fit in order to defeat the war-making state or enforce the said decision as speedily and effectively as possible.

In any case provided for by the foregoing article every member of the League will, if and so far as requested to do so by the Council, immediately subject the offending state to the severance of trade and financial relations, the prohibition of intercourse between its nationals and the nationals of the offending state, and the prevention of all financial, commercial, or personal intercourse between the nationals of such state and those of any other state.[2]

The use of the combined force in any particular case would, of course, be determined according to the actual circumstances. No real difficulty of principle arises in this connection. But the following observations of Herr Erzberger may serve to illustrate the subject :

' As soon as any League State is, from a military

[1] It may, however, prove more convenient to deal with air forces separately ; see pp. 186–188 *supra*.

[2] This clause is merely an adaptation of parts of Article 16 of the existing Covenant.

point of view, in a dangerous position, the League will take all preliminary measures, such as strengthening the frontier garrisons, or calling up the contingents from the several federated states, &c. At the first sign of invasion or bombardment of federated territory, these forces will invade the enemy's territory, even although there has been no formal declaration of war. . . . In the event of the hostile action against the League of a League State or an outside state extending to the sea, a fleet composed of units from the nations of the League would come into being. This fleet would have as its object, not only the destruction of the enemy fleet, but also the establishment of free maritime intercourse between the nations of the League. The League of Nations therefore will have far more effective means at its disposal than the present system of armaments ; it will have more authority than all the war lords in the world ; it will always be able to enforce its will. No nation which joins the League need have any fear that the laws of the League, or the awards of the Court of Arbitration, will not be enforced or fulfilled.' [1]

CONSTITUTION OF THE LEAGUE

The existence of the League is largely due to the general recognition of the fact that the preservation of peace—a pre-eminently moral object—can be secured only by the instrumentality of regulated force. The authority of the League and the obligatory effect of the decrees of its executive

[1] *The League of Nations*, English translation, at pp. 283, 287, 288.

14

must depend upon the power by which they are generally believed to be supported.

If the constitution of the League—after the suggested enlargement of its functions had been effected—rendered it possible, in an emergency calling for the immediate application of force, for the Great Powers to be outvoted by the smaller states—if action might be decreed against their will, or vetoed in spite of their belief that it was essential—there would be a continual danger of a want of coincidence between the influence attaching to the real strength of the Powers and the conventional authority of the League, which would strain the organization to the breaking-point.

In this matter there is no conflict whatever between expediency and justice. We have seen above that the theory of the equality of all states has no foundation either in fact or in moral principles. And any attempt to insist upon the realization of this conception in practice, while it would tend to retard the general advance of civilization, would particularly jeopardize the little states themselves. Only in peace maintained by the Powers can there be any security for their separate existence, and only by the disregard of the dogma of equality can peace be so maintained.

The primacy of the Great Powers is therefore justified by the necessity of the case as well as by the burden which they must undertake in supplying the forces required for the maintenance of peace. The fundamental difference between their position and that of the smaller states is of decisive importance in connexion with the exercise of the extended authority which, it is suggested, should be confided to the League.

In considering the distribution of the new functions of the League between its principal organs, an important distinction is to be borne in mind. Some of these functions directly and immediately concern the preservation of peace by measures which from time to time may be necessary to prevent or overcome any belligerent operations carried on without the authority of the League. Others concern disputes where the decision may involve an alteration of the *status quo*.

It appears evident from considerations which have been dealt with above that a body in which the Great Powers have a preponderating voice is alone fitted to be entrusted with the former class of functions. The success of the League in cases where these have to be brought into action must, moreover, to a great extent depend upon their exercise by a body comparatively small in number as well as representative of decisive power. On the other hand, where the latter class of functions are to be exercised, this smaller body may well share its authority with a larger. In these cases, accordingly, regard for justice in circumstances which may be difficult and doubtful, and the fact that the exigencies of the situation in which they arise will not normally preclude the opportunity for ample deliberation, would seem to render it desirable that all the Members of the League should take part in the proceedings which lead to an operative decision.

In the Council and the Assembly the League already possesses the two essential bodies. But the effective working of a reconstituted and fully efficient League of Peace would involve some alterations in their respective constitutional powers and methods of procedure.

It would probably not be profitable to discuss these alterations at any length in this place. But two considerations may perhaps usefully be hazarded in this connexion.

Executive functions are best performed by a body the members of which are not sufficiently numerous for the encouragement in their deliberations of argumentative debate as distinguished from the concise interchange of counsel. Experience, accordingly, seems to indicate that the number of members of such a body should not largely exceed twelve.

The requirement of a unanimous vote for the validity of a resolution of any body charged with the exercise of functions in the general interest of those whom its members represent is inconsistent with its complete efficiency. But no recognized principle is available for determining by what kind of majority such a body should be made capable of acting. Views as to what is practically best in this connexion will accordingly vary very widely. All, however, will agree that, having regard to the difficulty and gravity of the issues involved in international disputes, it is of paramount importance that, when the League takes action with regard to them, it should carry with it a great preponderance of the public opinion of the world. At the same time it is to be borne in mind that no society can conduct its affairs satisfactorily if a relatively very small number of individuals can prevent a course of action which all the others consider necessary in the general interest.

After long ages of the travail of humanity the League of Nations has been nobly born. May it grow in wisdom and in stature and in the favour which can alone secure the fulness of its living power ! For, until mankind have won their way to a stage upon their upward journey far higher than that which they have hitherto attained—until the world has been redeemed from egoism, cruelty, and strife—the purpose of this League will never fail, nor should the sceptre fall from its hands.

In the supreme tribunal of the British Empire there was, until the early years of this century, always a vacant place at the head of the table, along the two sides of which were ranged the judges who were to decide the pending suit. It was left to the imagination of the litigants and their advocates to envisage the august figure for whom that place was theoretically reserved. In the Council and Assembly of the League of Nations every chair is occupied by a representative of one of the states of the world. But it may well be devoutly hoped that there will always be room for the presence of the spirit of goodwill as the presiding genius in the citadel of peace.

PROPOSITION XXI.—In order that the League of Nations may fulfil its purpose, it must provide an authority empowered to determine in the last resort every dispute which may threaten a disturbance of the peace.

APPENDIX

THE COVENANT OF THE LEAGUE OF NATIONS

THE HIGH CONTRACTING PARTIES,

In order to promote international co-operation and to achieve international peace and security

 by the acceptance of obligations not to resort to war,

 by the prescription of open, just and honourable relations between nations,

 by the firm establishment of the understandings of international law as the actual rule of conduct among Governments,

 and by the maintenance of justice and a scrupulous respect for all treaty obligations in the dealings of organized peoples with one another,

Agree to this Covenant of the League of Nations.

ARTICLE I

1. The original Members of the League of Nations shall be those of the Signatories which are named in the Annex to this Covenant and also such of those other States named in the Annex as shall accede without reservation to this Covenant. Such accession shall be effected by a Declaration deposited with the Secretariat within two months of the coming into force of the

Covenant. Notice thereof shall be sent to all other Members of the League.

2. Any fully self-governing State, Dominion or Colony not named in the Annex may become a Member of the League if its admission is agreed to by two-thirds of the Assembly, provided that it shall give effective guarantees of its sincere intention to observe its international obligations, and shall accept such regulations as may be prescribed by the League in regard to its military, naval and air forces and armaments.

3. Any Member of the League may, after two years' notice of its intention so to do, withdraw from the League, provided that all its international obligations and all its obligations under this Covenant shall have been fulfilled at the time of its withdrawal.

ARTICLE 2

The action of the League under this Covenant shall be effected through the instrumentality of an Assembly and of a Council, with a permanent Secretariat.

ARTICLE 3

1. The Assembly shall consist of Representatives of the Members of the League.

2. The Assembly shall meet at stated intervals and from time to time as occasion may require at the Seat of the League or at such other place as may be decided upon.

3. The Assembly may deal at its meetings with any matter within the sphere of action of the League or affecting the peace of the world.

4. At meetings of the Assembly, each Member of the League shall have one vote, and may have not more than three Representatives.

ARTICLE 4

1. The Council shall consist of Representatives of the Principal Allied and Associated Powers,[a] together with Representatives of four other Members of the League. These four Members of the League shall be selected by the Assembly from time to time in its discretion. Until the appointment of the Representatives of the four Members of the League first selected by the Assembly, Representatives of Belgium, Brazil, Spain and Greece shall be members of the Council.

2. With the approval of the majority of the Assembly, the Council may name additional Members of the League whose Representatives shall always be Members of the Council;[b] the Council with like approval may increase the number of Members of the League to be selected by the Assembly for representation on the Council.[c]

2 bis.* *The Assembly shall fix by a two-thirds majority the rules dealing with the election of the non-permanent Members of the Council, and particularly such regulations as relate to their term of office and the conditions of re-eligibility.*

3. The Council shall meet from time to time as occasion may require, and at least once a year, at the Seat of the League, or at such other place as may be decided upon.

a. The Principal Allied and Associated Powers are the following: The United States of America, the British Empire, France, Italy and Japan.

b. In virtue of this paragraph of the Covenant, Germany was nominated as a permanent Member of the Council on September 8th, 1926.

c. The number of Members of the Council selected by the Assembly was increased to six instead of four by virtue of a resolution adopted at the Third ordinary meeting of the Assembly on September 25th, 1922. By a resolution taken by the Assembly on September 8th, 1926, the number of Members of the Council selected by the Assembly was increased to nine.

* This Amendment came into force on July 29th, 1926.

4. The Council may deal at its meetings with any matter within the sphere of action of the League or affecting the peace of the world.

5. Any Member of the League not represented on the Council shall be invited to send a Representative to sit as a member at any meeting of the Council during the consideration of matters specially affecting the interests of that Member of the League.

6. At meetings of the Council, each Member of the League represented on the Council shall have one vote, and may have not more than one Representative.

ARTICLE 5

1. Except where otherwise expressly provided in this Covenant or by the terms of the present Treaty, decisions at any meeting of the Assembly or of the Council shall require the agreement of all the Members of the League represented at the meeting.

2. All matters of procedure at meetings of the Assembly or of the Council, including the appointment of Committees to investigate particular matters, shall be regulated by the Assembly or by the Council and may be decided by a majority of the Members of the League represented at the meeting.

3. The first meeting of the Assembly, and the first meeting of the Council shall be summoned by the President of the United States of America.

ARTICLE 6

1. The permanent Secretariat shall be established at the Seat of the League. The Secretariat shall comprise a Secretary-General and such secretaries and staff as may be required.

2. The first Secretary-General shall be the person named in the Annex ; thereafter the Secretary-General

shall be appointed by the Council with the approval of the majority of the Assembly.

3. The secretaries and staff of the Secretariat shall be appointed by the Secretary-General with the approval of the Council.

4. The Secretary-General shall act in that capacity at all meetings of the Assembly and of the Council.

5.* *The expenses of the League shall be borne by the Members of the League in the proportion decided by the Assembly.*

ARTICLE 7

1. The Seat of the League is established at Geneva.

2. The Council may at any time decide that the Seat of the League shall be established elsewhere.

3. All positions under or in connection with the League, including the Secretariat, shall be open equally to men and women.

4. Representatives of the Members of the League and officials of the League when engaged on the business of the League shall enjoy diplomatic privileges and immunities.

5. The buildings and other property occupied by the League or its officials or by Representatives attending its meetings shall be inviolable.

ARTICLE 8

1. The Members of the League recognise that the maintenance of peace requires the reduction of national armaments to the lowest point consistent with national

---

* This Amendment came into force on August 13th, 1924, and replaces the following paragraph :

' 5. The expenses of the Secretariat shall be borne by the Members of the League in accordance with the apportionment of the expenses of the International Bureau of the Universal Postal Union.'

safety and the enforcement by common action of international obligations.

2. The Council, taking account of the geographical situation and circumstances of each State, shall formulate plans for such reduction for the consideration and action of the several Governments.

3. Such plans shall be subject to reconsideration and revision at least every ten years.

4. After these plans shall have been adopted by the several Governments, the limits of armaments therein fixed shall not be exceeded without the concurrence of the Council.

5. The Members of the League agree that the manufacture by private enterprise of munitions and implements of war is open to grave objections. The Council shall advise how the evil effects attendant upon such manufacture can be prevented, due regard being had to the necessities of those Members of the League which are not able to manufacture the munitions and implements of war necessary for their safety.

6. The Members of the League undertake to interchange full and frank information as to the scale of their armaments, their military, naval and air programmes and the condition of such of their industries as are adaptable to warlike purposes.

ARTICLE 9

A permanent Commission shall be constituted to advise the Council on the execution of the provisions of Articles 1 and 8 and on military, naval and air questions generally.

ARTICLE 10

The Members of the League undertake to respect and preserve as against external aggression the territorial integrity and existing political independence of all

Members of the League. In case of any such aggression or in case of any threat or danger of such aggression the Council shall advise upon the means by which this obligation shall be fulfilled.

ARTICLE 11

1. Any war or threat of war, whether immediately affecting any of the Members of the League or not, is hereby declared a matter of concern to the whole League, and the League shall take any action that may be deemed wise and effectual to safeguard the peace of nations. In case any such emergency should arise the Secretary-General shall on the request of any Member of the League forthwith summon a meeting of the Council.

2. It is also declared to be the friendly right of each Member of the League to bring to the attention of the Assembly or of the Council any circumstance whatever affecting international relations which threatens to disturb international peace or the good understanding between nations upon which peace depends.

ARTICLE 12 *

1. The Members of the League agree that if there should arise between them any dispute likely to lead to

* The Amendments printed in italics relating to these Articles came into force on September 26th, 1924, and replace the following texts :

' ARTICLE 12

' The Members of the League agree that if there should arise between them any dispute likely to lead to a rupture they will submit the matter either to arbitration or to enquiry by the Council, and they agree in no case to resort to war until three months after the award by the arbitrators or the report by the Council.

' In any case under this Article the award of the arbitrators a rupture they will submit the matter either to arbitration *or judicial settlement* or to enquiry by the Council, and they agree in no case to resort to war until three months after the award by the arbitrators *or the judicial decision* or the report by the Council.

2. In any case under this Article the award of the arbitrators *or the judicial decision* shall be made within a reasonable time, and the report of the Council shall be made within six months after the submission of the dispute.

ARTICLE 13

1. The Members of the League agree that whenever any dispute shall arise between them which they recog-

shall be made within a reasonable time, and the report of the Council shall be made within six months after the submission of the dispute.'

' ARTICLE 13

' The Members of the League agree that whenever any dispute shall arise between them which they recognise to be suitable for submission to arbitration and which cannot be satisfactorily settled by diplomacy, they will submit the whole subject-matter to arbitration.

' Disputes as to the interpretation of a treaty, as to any question of international law, as to the existence of any fact which if established would constitute a breach of any international obligation, or as to the extent and nature of the reparation to be made for any such breach, are declared to be among those which are generally suitable for submission to arbitration.

' For the consideration of any such dispute, the court of arbitration to which the case is referred shall be the court agreed on by the parties to the dispute or stipulated in any convention existing between them.

' The Members of the League agree that they will carry out in full good faith any award that may be rendered and that they will not resort to war against a Member of the League which complies therewith. In the event of any failure to carry out such an award, the Council shall propose what steps should be taken to give effect thereto.'

nise to be suitable for submission to arbitration *or judicial settlement,* and which cannot be satisfactorily settled by diplomacy, they will submit the whole subject-matter to arbitration *or judicial settlement.*

2. Disputes as to the interpretation of a treaty, as to any question of international law, as to the existence of any fact which, if established would constitute a breach of any international obligation, or as to the extent and nature of the reparation to be made for any such breach, are declared to be among those which are generally suitable for submission to arbitration *or judicial settlement.*

3. *For the consideration of any such dispute, the court to which the case is referred shall be the Permanent Court of International Justice, established in accordance with Article 14, or any tribunal agreed on by the parties to the dispute or stipulated in any convention existing between them.*

4. The Members of the League agree that they will carry out in full good faith any award *or decision* that may be rendered, and that they will not resort to war against a Member of the League which complies therewith. In the event of any failure to carry out such an award *or decision,* the Council shall propose what steps should be taken to give effect thereto.

ARTICLE 14

The Council shall formulate and submit to the Members of the League for adoption plans for the establishment of a Permanent Court of International Justice. The Court shall be competent to hear and determine any dispute of an international character which the parties thereto submit to it. The Court may also give an advisory opinion upon any dispute or question referred to it by the Council or by the Assembly.

ARTICLE 15

1.* If there should arise between Members of the League any dispute likely to lead to a rupture, which is not submitted to arbitration *or judicial settlement* in accordance with Article 13, the Members of the League agree that they will submit the matter to the Council. Any party to the dispute may effect such submission by giving notice of the existence of the dispute to the Secretary-General, who will make all necessary arrangements for a full investigation and consideration thereof.

2. For this purpose the parties to the dispute will communicate to the Secretary-General, as promptly as possible, statements of their case with all the relevant facts and papers, and the Council may forthwith direct the publication thereof.

3. The Council shall endeavour to effect a settlement of the dispute, and if such efforts are successful, a statement shall be made public giving such facts and explanations regarding the dispute and the terms of settlement thereof as the Council may deem appropriate.

4. If the dispute is not thus settled, the Council either unanimously or by a majority vote shall make and publish a report containing a statement of the facts of

* The Amendment to the first paragraph of this Article came into force on September 26th, 1924, and replaces the following text :

' ARTICLE 15

' If there should arise between Members of the League any dispute likely to lead to a rupture, which is not submitted to arbitration in accordance with Article 13, the members of the League agree that they will submit the matter to the Council. Any party to the dispute may effect such submission by giving notice of the existence of the dispute to the Secretary-General, who will make all necessary arrangements for a full investigation and consideration thereof.'

the dispute and the recommendations which are deemed just and proper in regard thereto.

5. Any Member of the League represented on the Council may make public a statement of the facts of the dispute and of its conclusions regarding the same.

6. If a report by the Council is unanimously agreed to by the members thereof other than the Representatives of one or more of the parties to the dispute, the Members of the League agree that they will not go to war with any party to the dispute which complies with the recommendations of the report.

7. If the Council fails to reach a report which is unanimously agreed to by the members thereof, other than the Representatives of one or more of the parties to the dispute, the Members of the League reserve to themselves the right to take such action as they shall consider necessary for the maintenance of right and justice.

8. If the dispute between the parties is claimed by one of them, and is found by the Council to arise out of a matter which by international law is solely within the domestic jurisdiction of that party, the Council shall so report, and shall make no recommendation as to its settlement.

9. The Council may in any case under this Article refer the dispute to the Assembly. The dispute shall be so referred at the request of either party to the dispute provided that such request be made within fourteen days after the submission of the dispute to the Council.

10. In any case referred to the Assembly, all the provisions of this Article and of Article 12 relating to the action and powers of the Council shall apply to the action and powers of the Assembly, provided that a report made by the Assembly, if concurred in by the Representatives of those Members of the League represented on the Council and of a majority of the other Members of the League, exclusive in each case of the Representatives of

15

the parties to the dispute, shall have the same force as a report by the Council concurred in by all the members thereof other than the Representatives of one or more of the parties to the dispute.

ARTICLE 16

1. Should any Member of the League resort to war in disregard of its covenants under Articles 12, 13 or 15, it shall *ipso facto* be deemed to have committed an act of war against all other Members of the League, which hereby undertake immediately to subject it to the severance of all trade or financial relations, the prohibition of all intercourse between their nationals and the nationals of the covenant-breaking State, and the prevention of all financial, commercial, or personal intercourse between the nationals of the covenant-breaking State and the nationals of any other State, whether a Member of the League or not.

2. It shall be the duty of the Council in such case to recommend to the several Governments concerned what effective military, naval, or air force the Members of the League shall severally contribute to the armed forces to be used to protect the covenants of the League.

3. The Members of the League agree, further, that they will mutually support one another in the financial and economic measures which are taken under this Article, in order to minimise the loss and inconvenience resulting from the above measures, and that they will mutually support one another in resisting any special measures aimed at one of their number by the covenant-breaking State, and that they will take the necessary steps to afford passage through their territory to the forces of any of the Members of the League which are co-operating to protect the covenants of the League.

4. Any Member of the League which has violated any

covenant of the League may be declared to be no longer a Member of the League by a vote of the Council concurred in by the Representatives of all the other Members of the League represented thereon.

ARTICLE 17

1. In the event of a dispute between a Member of the League and a State which is not a Member of the League, or between States not Members of the League, the State or States not Members of the League shall be invited to accept the obligations of membership in the League for the purposes of such dispute, upon such conditions as the Council may deem just. If such invitation is accepted, the provisions of Articles 12 to 16 inclusive shall be applied with such modifications as may be deemed necessary by the Council.

2. Upon such invitation being given the Council shall immediately institute an inquiry into the circumstances of the dispute and recommend such action as may seem best and most effectual in the circumstances.

3. If a State so invited shall refuse to accept the obligations of membership in the League for the purposes of such dispute, and shall resort to war against a Member of the League, the provisions of Article 16 shall be applicable as against the State taking such action.

4. If both parties to the dispute when so invited refuse to accept the obligations of membership in the League for the purposes of such dispute, the Council may take such measures and make such recommendations as will prevent hostilities and will result in the settlement of the dispute.

ARTICLE 18

Every treaty or international engagement entered into hereafter by any Member of the League shall be forthwith registered with the Secretariat and shall as soon as possible be published by it. No such treaty or international engagement shall be binding until so registered.

ARTICLE 19

The Assembly may from time to time advise the reconsideration by Members of the League of treaties which have become inapplicable and the consideration of international conditions whose continuance might endanger the peace of the world.

ARTICLE 20

1. The Members of the League severally agree that this Covenant is accepted as abrogating all obligations or understandings *inter se* which are inconsistent with the terms thereof, and solemnly undertake that they will not hereafter enter into any engagements inconsistent with the terms thereof.

2. In case any Member of the League shall, before becoming a Member of the League, have undertaken any obligations inconsistent with the terms of this Covenant, it shall be the duty of such Member to take immediate steps to procure its release from such obligations.

ARTICLE 21

Nothing in this Covenant shall be deemed to affect the validity of international engagements, such as treaties of arbitration or regional understandings like the Monroe doctrine, for securing the maintenance of peace.

ARTICLE 22

1. To those colonies and territories which as a consequence of the late war have ceased to be under the

sovereignty of the States which formerly governed them and which are inhabited by peoples not yet able to stand by themselves under the strenuous conditions of the modern world, there should be applied the principle that the well-being and development of such peoples form a sacred trust of civilisation and that securities for the performance of this trust should be embodied in this Covenant.

2. The best method of giving practical effect to this principle is that the tutelage of such peoples should be entrusted to advanced nations who by reason of their resources, their experience or their geographical position can best undertake this responsibility, and who are willing to accept it, and that this tutelage should be exercised by them as Mandatories on behalf of the League.

3. The character of the mandate must differ according to the stage of the development of the people, the geographical situation of the territory, its economic conditions and other similar circumstances.

4. Certain communities formerly belonging to the Turkish Empire have reached a stage of development where their existence as independent nations can be provisionally recognised subject to the rendering of administrative advice and assistance by a Mandatory until such time as they are able to stand alone. The wishes of these communities must be a principal consideration in the selection of the Mandatory.

5. Other peoples, especially those of Central Africa, are at such a stage that the Mandatory must be responsible for the administration of the territory under conditions which will guarantee freedom of conscience and religion, subject only to the maintenance of public order and morals, the prohibition of abuses such as the slave trade, the arms traffic and the liquor traffic, and the prevention of the establishment of fortifications or

military and naval bases and of military training of the natives for other than police purposes and the defence of territory, and will also secure equal opportunities for the trade and commerce of other Members of the League.

6. There are territories, such as South-West Africa and certain of the South Pacific Islands, which, owing to the sparseness of their population, or their small size, or their remoteness from the centres of civilisation, or their geographical contiguity to the territory of the Mandatory, and other circumstances, can be best administered under the laws of the Mandatory as integral portions of its territory, subject to the safeguards above mentioned in the interests of the indigenous population.

7. In every case of mandate, the Mandatory shall render to the Council an annual report in reference to the territory committed to its charge.

8. The degree of authority, control, or administration to be exercised by the Mandatory shall, if not previously agreed upon by the Members of the League, be explicitly defined in each case by the Council.

9. A permanent Commission shall be constituted to receive and examine the annual reports of the Mandatories and to advise the Council on all matters relating to the observance of the mandates.

ARTICLE 23

Subject to and in accordance with the provisions of international conventions existing or hereafter to be agreed upon, the Members of the League :

(a) will endeavour to secure and maintain fair and humane conditions of labour for men, women, and children, both in their own countries and in all countries to which their commercial and industrial relations extend, and for that purpose will establish and maintain the necessary international organisations ;

(b) undertake to secure just treatment of the native inhabitants of territories under their control ;

(c) will entrust the League with the general supervision over the execution of agreements with regard to the traffic in women and children, and the traffic in opium and other dangerous drugs ;

(d) will entrust the League with the general supervision of the trade in arms and ammunition with the countries in which the control of this traffic is necessary in the common interest ;

(e) will make provision to secure and maintain freedom of communications and of transit and equitable treatment for the commerce of all Members of the League. In this connection, the special necessities of the regions devastated during the war of 1914–1918 shall be borne in mind ;

(f) will endeavour to take steps in matters of international concern for the prevention and control of disease.

ARTICLE 24

1. There shall be placed under the direction of the League all international bureaux already established by general treaties if the parties to such treaties consent. All such international bureaux and all commissions for the regulation of matters of international interest hereafter constituted shall be placed under the direction of the League.

2. In all matters of international interest which are regulated by general conventions but which are not placed under the control of international bureaux or commissions, the Secretariat of the League shall, subject to the consent of the Council and if desired by the parties, collect and distribute all relevant information

and shall render any other assistance which may be necessary or desirable.

3. The Council may include as part of the expenses of the Secretariat the expenses of any bureau or commission which is placed under the direction of the League.

ARTICLE 25

The Members of the League agree to encourage and promote the establishment and co-operation of duly authorised voluntary national Red Cross organisations having as purposes the improvement of health, the prevention of disease and the mitigation of suffering throughout the world.

ARTICLE 26

1. Amendments to this Covenant will take effect when ratified by the Members of the League whose Representatives compose the Council and by a majority of the Members of the League whose Representatives compose the Assembly.

2. No such amendments shall bind any Member of the League which signifies its dissent therefrom, but in that case it shall cease to be a Member of the League.

INDEX

PRINTED BY MORRISON AND GIBB LTD., LONDON AND EDINBURGH

For Product Safety Concerns and Information please contact our EU
representative GPSR@taylorandfrancis.com
Taylor & Francis Verlag GmbH, Kaufingerstraße 24, 80331 München, Germany

www.ingramcontent.com/pod-product-compliance
Lightning Source LLC
Chambersburg PA
CBHW070353270326
41926CB00014B/2525

*9 7 8 0 3 6 7 1 4 3 7 5 6 *